THE ART OF
QUARTET
PLAYING

THE ART OF
QUARTET
PLAYING

The Guarneri Quartet
in Conversation with
David Blum

Alfred A. Knopf   New York   1986

Library of Congress Cataloging-in-Publication Data

Blum, David 1935–
The art of quartet playing.

Discography: p.
Includes index.
1. Ensemble playing. 2. String quartets—
Interpretation (phrasing, dynamics, etc.)
3. Guarneri Quartet. 4. Musicians—United States—Interviews.
5. Beethoven, Ludwig van, 1770–1827. Quartets, strings,
no. 14, op. 131, C♯ minor. I. Title.
MT728.B6 1986   785.7′0471   85-45796
ISBN 0-394-53985-0

Do you think I worry about your lousy fiddle
when the spirit speaks to me?

Beethoven to Schuppanzigh, in response
to his complaint about difficulties encountered
when playing one of the quartets

CONTENTS

PREFACE

This book is a study in depth of the art of string quartet playing. The members of the Guarneri Quartet have brought to this work their experience both as individuals and as an ensemble of twenty years' duration. They share here the exploration into interpretation to which each of them is passionately committed; they open the door to their workshop so that the reader may closely observe the process by which a performance is shaped.

Most of the material is dealt with in round-table discussions. Although I have arranged it in categories, all is interrelated; aspects of technique are invariably dealt with as means to expressive ends. As with all outstanding artists, the Quartet members' musical conceptions are powerful, deeply rooted, and occasionally unconventional. If their views are sometimes expressed in highly subjective ways, this is only as it should be.

A quartet can be no stronger than the individuals who compose it; I have therefore asked each player—a consummate instrumentalist in his own right—to tell something of his own background of studies and precepts of teaching. These interviews, entitled "Four Voices," begin with David Soyer and build from the cello upwards; they inevitably encompass essential principles of string playing in general. (A short glossary may be found at the back of the book for the benefit of those readers not acquainted with string-playing terminology.)

In selecting Beethoven's Quartet in C-sharp minor for detailed study in the final chapter, the Quartet pays homage to a supreme masterpiece while at the same time drawing together many strands of the book in relation to the interpretation of a single work.

My first encounter with a member of the Guarneri Quartet occurred in 1952 when I formed a young players' chamber orchestra in Los Angeles in which Arnold Steinhardt took part. I was sixteen at the time, Arnold fifteen. Twelve years later—just prior to the Quartet's formation—I had the pleasure of welcoming both John Dalley and Arnold as participants in the Esterhazy Orchestra during its first American tour, Arnold performing as soloist. I made the friendship of David Soyer and Michael Tree at Marlboro in the early 1960s.

Two decades later I suggested to the Quartet players that we create this book together. For that purpose, I accompanied them on tours in America and Europe. The conversations took place in hotels, motels, restaurants, green rooms, airplanes, trains, and cars (all five of us plus instruments and luggage packed into a single vehicle speeding across the Arizona desert); on occasion we were able to meet in the tranquility of my home near Geneva.

My work on this book was greatly eased by the fact that the members of the Guarneri Quartet remain good-natured in their mutual relationships to an extent that is rare for any chamber-music ensemble, much less for one of such exceptional longevity. This is due above all to the deep and abiding respect each player has for his colleagues. They know too that good relations in the personal as in the artistic realm don't always come of themselves, but must be worked for. They find it important to preserve their independence as much as possible. Summers are reserved exclusively for their families, and when on tour, they often travel separately and stay in different hotels. John Dalley, the most introverted of the four (though not so on the concert platform), will sometimes disappear entirely between concerts, mysteriously surfacing again at the appointed hour.

At rehearsals criticism is meted out equally by each member with a frankness that would far surpass the level of tolerance within most other ensembles. Yet the atmosphere is astonishingly free of tension. At times a point may be stubbornly argued, but the overriding spirit is one of patience and open-mindedness. A typical Guarneri rehearsal on tour takes place in a motel room, music strewn over beds and chairs, Michael Tree in tennis garb, and all the players in the most casual and unlikely poses for serious music making. Yet once bow touches string, they give the task in hand their total concentration. A piece revived from their past repertoire will be played through from first note to last and commented upon wherever necessary. But most revelatory is the way in which these rehearsals preserve a sense of musical continuity. Despite the frequent stopping and starting, one doesn't feel that the flow of the work is substantially interrupted. A ritardando or moment of rubato may sometimes be referred to as "excessive" but then not gone over again; the players can rely upon their innate taste and years of experience in working together to give the passage its just proportions in performance. The piece emerges from the rehearsal *à point,* carefully restudied and ready to be fully savored on the concert stage.

A striking characteristic of these four musicians is their individual and collective sense of humor, which, given the difficulties inherent in two decades of touring and the presentation of over two thousand concerts, provides a blessed relief from stress. Jokes are traded around the clock—gentle or satiric, witty or corny, at all events irresistible and the bane of the Quartet's interviewer.

The joyous play on words, the natural high spirits, the ebullience typical of the daily life of the Guarneri Quartet find a parallel in their music making. The players' technical command and level of musical development allow them to enjoy a measure of freedom at the heights, to disport with the music—not arbitrarily and irreverently, but creatively and imaginatively, in the spirit and at the service of the artwork. One is reminded of Schiller: "Man is completely human only when he is at play"—a truth that strikes home time and again in Guarneri Quartet performances, whether in the banter of the Presto from Beethoven's Opus 130, the yearning of the Adagio from Schumann's A-minor Quartet, the passion of the Finale of Beethoven's Opus 132, or the mystery of the pianissimo passages in the first movement of Schubert's G-major Quartet that quietly herald the formation of a new cosmos.

For the Guarneri Quartet every work is a living entity; no two performances are exactly alike. Their conceptions are always evolving. For this reason their interpretative markings (enclosed within parentheses in the music examples) should not be regarded as definitive but as expressions of the moment, subject to variations in light and shade.

Despite the exceptional skill the players bring to a performance, they don't speak of "perfection," a concept they find sterile. They readily admit that other quartets look for and achieve a more consistent blend of timbre and unity of style. They enter into the music's expressive stream and let it work upon them, even if, in so doing, an occasional rough edge appears. Their goal is always to communicate the music as a living experience.

I have been privileged to attend many Guarneri Quartet concerts over the years, but even so I was not prepared for the impact of their complete Beethoven cycle in the concert hall. (I heard it for the first time in Geneva in 1983.) Here and there I might have preferred a different approach to a particular tempo or phrasing, but it would be hard to equal the overall level of commitment, the expressive continuity, the perception of the music's dramaturgy, and, above all, the sense of spontaneous re-creation. The voice of Beethoven was heard, ever-present and unmistakable.

Unlikely marriages are sometimes the most successful. Who can explain the correlation of meticulous craftsmanship and audacious abandon characteristic of great artistry? In not restricting the improvisatory impulse, the Guarneri Quartet dares to catch it in flight, thus forging a unity at an ever higher level. But let it not be forgotten that the workshop of these four craftsmen provides the foundation without which no real spontaneity can take place.

John Dalley, who even makes the bows that he uses with such skill, is a modest, soft-spoken man with a way of coming directly to the point. One day in the early stages of our talks he said, "If anything is the hallmark of our performances it's that we like to take chances and avoid playing in a predictable way." I replied (with due caution), "Nothing is more creative than this spirit of improvisation—but, of course, within bounds." "We have no bounds," said Dalley, a twinkle in his eye.

In the words of William Blake, "No bird soars too high, if he soars with his own wings."

DAVID BLUM
Vandœuvres, Switzerland
May 1986

ACKNOWLEDGEMENTS

I wish to thank John, David, Arnold, and Michael for their unfailing patience, helpfulness, and good humor under sometimes hectic conditions. I am grateful to Peter Gras, Antony Hopkins, and Warren Stewart for their many valuable suggestions; to Peter Ammann, Joan Dickson, and Bernard Zaslav for their helpful advice; to Tabitha Collingbourne for preparing the music examples; and, at Knopf, to Carol Janeway and to Eva Resnikova, for having so carefully seen this book through production. My gratitude must be expressed publicly as well as privately to my wife, Sara, for her perceptive counsel given at every stage of the book's formulation.

THE ART OF
QUARTET
PLAYING

The Guarneri String Quartet

ARNOLD STEINHARDT, *first violin*

JOHN DALLEY, *second violin*

MICHAEL TREE, *viola*

DAVID SOYER, *cello*

COMPLEMENTS
AND
CHALLENGES

You each have a strong individual artistic temperament. You've nevertheless found the means to bring those temperaments together to forge a unity of conception in quartet playing. To what extent has this required a sacrifice of your independent musical personalities?

TREE   It may seem paradoxical, but I would say: not at all. There's a widespread belief that string-quartet playing demands a constant unanimity of style and approach. Yet it should be remembered that a quartet is based on four individual voices. The fact that we have to coordinate and find a proper balance doesn't mean that any one of us should become faceless. On the contrary; the re-creation of a masterpiece needs the full, vital participation of each of us.

DALLEY   Some quartets do give high priority to sacrificing individual differences; they work hard to blend together so that the four players sound as alike as possible. The results are sometimes admirable in their own way. However, our approach is quite different.

STEINHARDT   People sometimes come up to us after concerts and comment that it must have been difficult to find four musicians who think so alike on the subject of quartet playing. There's something of a contradiction in this. The more developed our musical personalities are, the less likely we are to think alike. In fact, I can't imagine four musicians more different from one another in certain ways than we are. For example, one would think that the first thing a quartet must establish is a uniform approach to vibrato. Yet each of our vibratos retains a distinctly personal quality; of course, we all place a high premium on *variety* of vibrato in its artistic application.

SOYER   The crux of the matter is that the unanimity of our approach in a performance is determined not by a preconceived philosophy of what string-quartet playing is supposed to be but by our musical conception of the work at hand. We're four musicians performing a single piece of music, and we come to a common opinion about that work.

DALLEY   Each piece will make its own demands; you can't put down a general rule about "blending." There are many passages which require a total blend, such as the beginning of the slow movement of Beethoven's Opus 132, where every degree of vibrato—or *non*vibrato—must be perfectly matched. But sometimes you have the opposite problem: that of blending too well. For instance, certain voices may not stand out in adequate relief. You also find that in orchestral playing. A certain sixteenth-note figure may sound fine when played by the violins but be less clearly heard when repeated by the cellos. The cellos are then obliged to articulate differently from the violins.

TREE   It's more of a true dialogue when two voices are distinct from each other. Obviously, the differences shouldn't be farfetched. If two of us play identical phrases, it shouldn't sound as if we're arguing. On the other hand, each player may well retain something of his own personality.

SOYER   Let's remember that each instrument in the quartet has its own character. If a violin figure is taken over by the viola, we don't necessarily feel that it must be played in exactly the same way. It's another register, another timbre; that difference is something which we look for rather than try to avoid.

Have your individual ways of playing come any closer together over the years?

STEINHARDT   I don't think they have. In fact, they may have moved further apart, because each of our musical personalities has continued to evolve in its own way. It's important that each of us go on his own musical voyage through life, whatever it may be.

Would you be willing to characterize your individual ways?

TREE   That's not fair.

DALLEY   It may be the end of the Guarneri String Quartet if we go into that.

SOYER   Well, it's easy. From highest instrument to lowest: bad, bad, bad, good.

STEINHARDT   Shouldn't we reverse the order? However, to put it discreetly: we complement and challenge one another. We value our differences; they bring added scope and dimension to our playing and allow each of us to grow—as in a good marriage.

TREE   All I can say is that after twenty years in the quartet, I'm happily surprised on occasion to find myself totally wrong about what I think a player will do, or how he'll react in a particular passage. I don't yet know enough about the others' temperaments—thank heaven—to be sure to read their thinking correctly. Any one of us might interpret a given phrase many times in a certain way and then play it quite differently without warning. There's a wonderful passage towards the end of the first movement of the Debussy Quartet where the second violin and the viola have to act as one player, but it's clearly John's place to shape the line as he wishes, since he has the upper voice.

Although it's marked "diminuendo," rises and falls are natural to the line as it descends, and there's great rhythmic leeway.

DALLEY   Debussy gives his blessing by marking "a tempo rubato," which allows one to make a fantasy of it rather than something concrete.

TREE   Now, in this passage John and I play a little unspoken game. He knows that he's throwing me curves, and that I sometimes have to stand on my head to catch them. But I've never once said, "John, let's rehearse that. Tell me what you want to do, and I'll try my damnedest to do it with you." I'd rather not play quartets at all than nail everything down in advance. There's rubato in every note; I have to try to climb into John's psyche. No two eighth notes are ever straight—nor should they be. At (a) the quarters may be elongated and the eighths flowing forward—or sometimes it's the reverse. John may make a crescendo at (c), but if he's already made a strong crescendo at (b), I can anticipate—knowing him—that he'll make a less apparent one at (c). As to the triplets at (d), he might bow them as marked, or perhaps he'll play them with separate bows at the point, or in a combination of the two. And I'm expected not merely to follow him but to react to him, which is a lot different from merely being an accompanist. Should I find myself committed to a bowing that he isn't doing at the moment, it's my job to make my phrasing sound similar to his, even if we aren't actually bowing in the same manner. Of course, if he ever felt that I couldn't meet the challenge, he would never endanger the performance. From time to time we'll all test one another somewhat—just as John will test me in that Debussy passage.

Well, for better or worse, that's a good example of the individuality we retain in the Guarneri String Quartet.

SOYER   We preserve our individual ways in our choices of instruments as well. People often have the idea that quartet instruments should be matched just as players should be matched. We're sometimes asked whether we as individuals take the quartet into consideration when we buy an instrument. Do we attempt to match its sound to that of the other instruments in the quartet so that all four players decide on whether the instrument is to be acquired? I'm afraid we don't.

DALLEY   It would place a restriction on our own playing, and the quartet would suffer in turn.

Yet as each of you is a soloist in his own right, wouldn't you naturally select an instrument that's well balanced—that doesn't overly emphasize one particular tone color?

TREE   That may be true. However, what I most object to is the designation "a good quartet violin"—implying that it's a sweet- and small-sounding instrument, intimate in quality and easy to combine with others, and therefore better suited to chamber music than to solo playing. This shows a lack of understanding of the demands put on string-quartet players.

STEINHARDT   As we have no orchestra or piano to project against, we more often use the softer side of the dynamic range—from *mp* to *ppp*. The instrument must therefore be able to respond immediately to the smallest gesture. But the instrument must also have power, depth, and brilliance, not least because you're surrounded by three vital players and you often have to cut through a dense texture.

TREE   When we play one of the large-scale Beethoven or Schubert quartets, we strain our instruments to the limit, and sometimes beyond. And we all have good instruments, I must say; they're all of solo quality. Yet it really shouldn't surprise us that such misunderstandings persist—even among professional musicians—because when we ourselves began to play together, it took a while for these things to seep in. I only gradually began to understand what string-quartet playing is all about.

When you rehearse, one sees the complementing and challenging process in action. It's like four sculptors working away at a stone from all sides, while keeping sufficient distance to envisage the whole.

DALLEY   We usually manage to reconcile the various viewpoints, I'm happy to say, but there are occasions when we don't. Unfortunately, a quartet is composed of an even number of players, and two against two creates an impasse. Obviously, one of the interpretations must then prevail; yet it's not as if it "wins out" for all time. It may seem to be the most reasonable or convincing for the moment, but that may change later on; there's a constant working-out process.

STEINHARDT   We're always amused when a local newspaper asks us for an interview, because the first question is usually, "How did you decide on the name of the quartet?" And we can't even agree on that! So how are we going to agree on phrasing or on anything else? But tomorrow we'll disagree in a slightly different way from today, so an evolution is always taking place. One mustn't forget that in developing a quartet, personal qualities play as important a role as musicianship; the two can't be easily separated. Each of us has to be strong enough to exert his leadership, strong enough to endure the constant criticism of his colleagues, and strong enough to let go of cherished ideas when they don't coincide with the majority opinion. Of course, every quartet will have a different set of interdynamics. One often finds disparities in the attitudes of the players. One player may be more flexible than another. In the heat of a performance the flexible person will tend to give in to the unyielding one. But then, in the next rehearsal, the flexible one should say to the other, "I was forced to follow you in this place but would prefer to play it differently."

The ideal situation is to have four people who are equally capable of leading or following.

TREE   Yes, exactly. I hope we can put to rest for all time the concept that a whole quartet must necessarily be dominated by a single player. It's usually thought to be the first violinist. In Europe—perhaps because traditions die harder there—they're less apt to do away with this notion. In Germany and Austria they refer to the "primarius"—an expression which surprised us when we first heard it—while in England they speak of the "leader" of a string quartet. The idea of a "primarius" is something that never would have occurred to us; it's antithetical to our way of thinking. When we're asked, "Where is the primarius?" we simply answer, "Which primarius? There are four of us." I feel that a group in which one person determines how the others should play doesn't sound the same as one in which every member is involved in the leadership and communicates musically on an equal basis.

STEINHARDT   Naturally, in any given passage there will usually be a leading voice, but that may be in any one of the four instruments. You don't assert your leadership just because you happen to be the first violinist.

DALLEY   For my part, I wouldn't be so absolute as to reject the idea of a "primarius" under all circumstances. Just from the standpoint of getting things done, a dictatorship—hopefully a benevolent one—can sometimes solve a lot of problems. That's not to say it's the best way, but some quartets do function that way and feel comfortable with it.

Our way entails more risk and is more difficult to put into effect, but it's worth the effort. Alexander Schneider, for many years second violinist of the Budapest Quartet, had a helpful idea as to how to instill a sense of democracy in action into young quartet players. He suggested letting a different member of the quartet take on responsibility for the evolution of each movement of a work. Should any questions be raised about interpretation, that player would have the deciding vote. In this way everyone has an opportunity at some time to assert his or her musical convictions but must at other times submit to another point of view.

One often finds the attitude that chamber music should mainly be played with discretion and restraint. This concept must have an inhibiting psychological effect on the player.

TREE   I'm glad you've touched upon that. It's the natural result of the misconception I spoke of. How often have you heard it said that he or she is a good violinist but is lacking in personality, projection, or even technique and would therefore be more suited to chamber music than to solo playing? The fact is that playing a great quartet, whether it be Beethoven or Bartók, requires an *excess* of temperament, of personal conviction, of technique. I went through all the rigors of a solo violin education, and demanding ones they were, because my teacher was a great violinist who insisted that all his students play the entire virtuoso literature—Vieuxtemps, Spohr, Ernst, Wieniawski, Paganini, Sarasate. I'm grateful for that today, and I would advise young string players who envisage a career playing quartets not to think it's sufficient to begin with Mozart quartets; one shouldn't neglect the major concertos and virtuoso works. In quartet playing there won't be as many gymnastics per minute, but the amount of technical control and variety of nuance that's needed is greater than what one normally finds in the solo repertoire. We're often called upon to do things that someone playing a Wieniawski concerto doesn't have to do, and those things happen to be among the hardest to achieve on the instrument: playing in an imitative manner, finding the ideal degree of color, cutting through textures. We can't just change bows as we would like or indulge ourselves technically as a concerto player would, because it might be out of context with what's going on around us. When you're onstage alone, you have greater leeway and fewer constraints placed on you. All of which is to say that you have to be a first-class instrumentalist to be a first-class string-quartet player.

STEINHARDT   The reticence one frequently finds in young quartet players often comes in part from their feeling intimidated by questions of ensemble. People tend to get very worried about the difficulty of playing together. Good ensemble is laudable, but I wouldn't put it first on my scale of priorities. I would rather hear a quartet play in tune than merely play together, and I would prefer by far to hear a fervent musical performance, even if the ensemble is sometimes a little dog-eared. But for many young players, perfection of ensemble becomes a kind of end-all. They work and work, and leave the rehearsal happy because they have played accurately together. That's really only the first step.

SOYER   But we mustn't be too critical. After all, when we began playing together, one of our chief concerns was to ensure our ensemble playing. A lot of effort was devoted to trying to obtain pinpoint accuracy. As the years have gone by, we've become less concerned about that, and we've also developed ways of achieving good ensemble without discussing it, or sometimes even rehearsing it.

You've achieved this largely by means of a fascinating and rather complex system of "leads"—that is, signals given by any one of you at critical junctures during the course of a movement—a system of which the audience is virtually unaware—enabling you to maintain a firm grip on the ensemble.

SOYER   That's an important factor, and it helps make it possible for us to play as a leaderless quartet.

DALLEY   And, as you say, most of the time our leads are not obvious to the public. They wonder how we manage to play together. They don't see Arnold making wild gestures or conducting as some first violinists do. Our leads are not any larger than they have to be, and, of course, they're spread around the quartet.

STEINHARDT   It's important not to allow our gestures to distract from the line of the music. Whether we like it or not, the audience takes in the visual aspect as part of the experience.

It's interesting to observe the way in which you divide the responsibility for leads among you. Did this system develop through trial and error?

STEINHARDT   Yes. We began with the conventional wisdom: if the first violin has the upper voice, he should give the lead; and if someone else has the melodic line, he will give the lead. But this doesn't take into account a great many circumstances which crop up so often that one can hardly even call them exceptional.

DALLEY   Let's say that Arnold is busy playing an expressive transitional passage going into a place that has to be led, and he finds it awkward to give the lead in the middle of all he has to do. Then I might say, "Why don't you just play it, and I'll lead here." Rather than being an encumbrance to Arnold and depriving him of the liberty of playing the transition exactly as he would wish, the fact that someone else gives the lead frees him to concentrate wholly on the music.

STEINHARDT   Naturally, in such a case John won't lead willfully; he'll do so in a way that's comfortable for me in that situation. We have to trust one another's judgment.

SOYER   Leads aren't always taken by the most seemingly obvious person. For instance, at the beginning of Beethoven's Opus 59, No. 1 [see page 57], although I have the melody, John gives the lead. This allows the second violin and the viola to establish the tempo of their eighth-note figure without difficulty and permits me to enter without having to concern myself with anything other than playing the melody.

TREE   The relationship of the viola and the cello is in many ways similar to that of the two violins. We often play melodic figures together—for instance, in thirds or sixths. In such cases, where I have the upper part, I'll usually lead, though naturally I'll defer to Dave if he has the leading voice.

DALLEY   We'll often ask Dave to lead in pizzicato passages. A cellist's preparatory motion for pizzicato is larger and slower than that of a violinist. It's much easier for us to follow him than for him to follow us.

What advice would you give players to ensure that a lead will be effective in producing good ensemble?

STEINHARDT   I feel that it's a good idea to give a strong lead and then follow everybody else. Of course, you have to be true to your own lead or the others won't trust you. But then, to ensure that everything will be all right, you have to listen carefully to make certain that the others are with you. Take, for instance, the Finale of Mozart's K. 589:

The ensemble here requires attention. After I give the lead, I'll watch the motion of John's bow and, if necessary, slightly alter my own motion so that we're perfectly together. When leading an entrance that involves the whole quartet—such as the majestic opening to Beethoven's Opus 127—I'll give a strongly assertive lead, meanwhile picking someone to watch—often Dave, as he has the bass. If two people are clearly in accord, the others sense it, and there's a greater chance of unanimity. We've never talked about this, but it's nonetheless something we've always done.

Do you usually lead with your bow?

STEINHARDT　Yes, with the bow or the violin—except when I'm already playing. A difficult situation arises when you're holding a long, sustained note and must yet lead the passage that follows. A gesture with the bow or the instrument might then distort the end of the note. In such cases you may need to nod your head or sniff; you could even use your knee if you had to. The most important thing is not the technical means; it's knowing the function of a good preparatory beat. The keys to a good lead are clarity and concision; I try to find the most natural unit of beat and give it with authority. Inexperienced players often give a rather sluggish lead because they're hesitant about the tempo.

SOYER　A tempo may be particularly difficult to fix in the inner ear when the notes at the beginning of a piece lack decisive rhythmic character. At such times it may be helpful to focus on a passage that comes later in the movement—a running figure or something that lends itself to easy tempo identification. Once one has that in mind, one can superimpose it over the opening bars. This is of particular importance, for instance, in many of Haydn's slow movements.

STEINHARDT　Sometimes one has to give two successive leads. The first bar of the Minuet of Beethoven's Opus 59, No. 3 looks deceptively simple—

—but the ensemble doesn't come as easily as in the fifth bar, where the second violin establishes the motion of sixteenth notes. Even the Budapest Quartet found the first bar tricky. I give an indication on the second beat in preparation for the third; I've developed a special tic for that bar.

　It's also important to decide what rhythmic unit you're going to choose for the upbeat. An Andante in $\frac{4}{4}$ could be led with either an eighth or a quarter note; the latter would probably be more suitable to convey a lyrical feeling. But it's hard to generalize. As a matter of fact, I don't always lead a given passage in the same way. In Beethoven's Opus 74, at the end of the slow movement [Adagio ma non troppo; $\frac{3}{8}$], where there are a lot of isolated notes separated by rests, I'll sometimes give a leisurely eighth-note preparatory beat, sometimes a sixteenth. Much depends on the mood of the moment.

SOYER   In passages where there are many rests, it's important that the sense of connection be sustained. This is both a physical and a mental process. During the exceptionally long silences in the slow movement of Beethoven's Opus 18, No. 1—

—you mustn't just collapse and wait for the next chord to come. In keeping with the diminuendo, we play the first two chords at the frog and the last two at the point. Directly after each chord we move our bows to the position needed for the subsequent chord, where they remain suspended in anticipation. We sustain the vibrato as long as possible. One should feel as if one is playing the silences.

TREE   The gesture should always be at one with the spirit of the music, whatever it may be. For example, when a movement starts lyrically, the preparatory beat should often seem more a continuation than a beginning. Sometimes the opposite is appropriate. I recall hearing a Koussevitzky concert when he began Tchaikovsky's Fourth Symphony by flinging his arms out of nowhere without any sort of preparation; the effect was electrifying.

Do you sometimes surprise one another like that?

STEINHARDT   Not intentionally. Surprises do come up from time to time, though, such as when John once gave a lead while I was reaching for my mute.

In an effort to improve ensemble, chamber-music players often make a point of looking at one another.

SOYER   We try to avoid that.

STEINHARDT   I haven't looked at these guys in years.

SOYER   Eye contact doesn't do any good, because you don't play with your eyes.

STEINHARDT   God has given us peripheral vision. That's enough for everything you need in a quartet. To actually look at John I would have to turn my back to the audience. I don't have to see his expression—inspiring as it may be—but I must be able to see his bow and, above all, the fingers of his left hand.

DALLEY   Alexander Schneider used to say that in order to achieve good ensemble, "You have to eat up the other person's fingers with your eyes."

STEINHARDT   Leaving aside the cannibalistic implications, that is useful advice.

SOYER   Many people who aren't greatly experienced in chamber music think that watching the bow is the thing to do. But bow movements can be deceptive. Sometimes you move your bow before it makes actual contact with the string, or sometimes the string doesn't speak immediately. The finger, however, normally strikes the string just when you play.

Of course, there are times—say, in the slow movement of Beethoven's Opus 132—when it's not really a question of watching the bow or the fingers; it's more a matter of feeling the pulse.

DALLEY   There's also a certain body language that each of us has when he plays. You get to know that about your colleagues and react accordingly. Over the years a great deal of it becomes intuitive.

SOYER   Our way of ensemble playing is not that someone leads and everyone else just follows. The actual lead may be in the first or second

fiddle, but, in fact, everyone feels it at the same time; everyone is thinking towards a central point: the start of a piece, a ritardando, or whatever
it may be. We don't follow each other; we play together. There's a difference in that. If it goes wrong, the disaster will be greater than if we had
followed the traditional method and taken fewer risks. But if it goes
well, it will be far better. It's not the safest way, but it's our way.

*In what respects would you say that your manner of working together has
evolved since the quartet was formed?*

TREE   One consideration that colored our thinking from the very beginning was the fact that we didn't have long months to sit together and
rehearse and learn each other's style of playing and philosophize over
music. One reads of quartets of the past who would rehearse for a year
before they dared play a note in public; there was almost a mystique
about quartet playing. Well, in our very first year, when we were in
residence at Harpur College in Binghamton, New York, we had to give
fifteen separate programs. That means we had to learn forty-five works.
Not only did we have no time to philosophize, but, as a matter of fact,
we had to place a limit on the amount of talk during rehearsals. That
kind of pragmatic view has held through the years and has influenced
the way in which we work. Of course, we say something if we feel we
have to, but I've known other groups who would talk us into the
ground.

STEINHARDT   We did, however, talk a great deal more at the beginning
than we do now. We were still at the time of life when we were taking
music apart in our minds for our own selves, not just as a quartet. Our
style of playing and rehearsing was certainly more self-conscious then
than it is now.

DALLEY   In our youthful ardor each of us would come to a rehearsal
carrying the banner for a particular aesthetic idea and was ready to fight
to the death for it.

SOYER   There was to be a ritardando here, an accelerando there, just as
you would sprinkle salt and pepper over a dish. We would waste a lot of
time struggling until something came out of it. We've since learned that
it sometimes doesn't matter whether a detail is painted lighter or darker;
each can be valid, and our feeling for these things changes constantly.
We no longer fight major battles over minor points.

STEINHARDT   This is, I think, a natural development. When a player first comes into a group, he feels he has to establish his own identity and his own area. I don't think we worry about that any more; everyone feels secure in his own position. Whatever I am, they all know it; and whatever they are, I know, too.

SOYER   Our style of playing has evolved towards greater continuity of rhythm and tempo. We try, nowadays, to avoid impositions and exaggerations. If one player takes a little musical liberty, the quartet goes along with him. We allow each other freedom—but there's a natural give and take.

Paradoxically, too much planned rubato can restrict true freedom.

SOYER   Precisely; there's a lack of spontaneity. A moment of ritardando or rubato should not sound contrived; it should be allowed to happen naturally.

One necessary consideration in quartet playing is, of course, the seating arrangement. How did you decide on the plan you have adopted—namely, from the audience's left to right: first violin, second violin, cello, and viola?

SOYER   We first tried the old European method of placing the cello on the outside facing the first violin, but I found it uncomfortable. The bass seemed to be in the wrong place. I feel that the bass should be at the back of the ensemble, where it will act as the foundation. It seemed strange to have the foundation up in front and to the side. Certain quartets of the last century, such as the Joachim Quartet, placed the cello at the back, even if the violins were divided on either side.

Have you ever tried dividing the violins?

DALLEY   No. There are many times when a composer will share a melodic line between the two violins in the same register; the timbres should be as similar as possible. We prefer that the violins sit next to each other so that the sound comes from the same direction. Thus we chose the only other possible arrangement, and that seems the most natural for us. Many quartets seat themselves this way; the Budapest did, for example.

In this arrangement isn't the viola the instrument most at a disadvantage, with its F-holes facing the back of the stage?

SOYER   Not in this quartet.

TREE   There are ways to get around the problem.

What are they?

TREE   Oh, I thought you wouldn't ask.

SOYER   To play very loudly is the way to get around it.

TREE   Well . . . at least in crucial or strategic places, one has to play a shade above the written dynamic level. And there's such a thing as defensive playing. I learned that during one of our first seasons, when Boris Kroyt, violist of the Budapest Quartet, joined us as second viola in a Brahms quintet, which meant that his sound was, even more than mine, directed towards the back of the stage. In the concert I nearly fell off of my chair, because the moment he had a solo, he wheeled around and almost stuck his scroll in my face to be sure his sound would project. It's amazing how much difference a slight turn can make. Arnold and I were once rehearsing Mozart's Sinfonia Concertante, and Isaac Stern, who was in the hall, told me, "Face more towards the audience." I turned the distance of a foot, so that the F-holes were pointed more directly towards the hall, and Isaac said the difference was striking.

   Apart from the slight acoustical handicap under which the viola suffers, our quartet arrangement is a very comfortable one. I am looking diagonally across at John, and I rely heavily on that; more often than not it's the second violinist who leads accompaniment figures, keeps things together, and holds the reins.

To what extent do acoustical considerations influence your performance?

DALLEY   Very little. People are often surprised when we don't rehearse in the hall on the day of a concert, but, frankly, we find it futile to do so.

SOYER   If we do go to a hall early, it's because we want to rehearse the pieces we're playing; it's not for acoustical purposes. First of all, the hall when empty will sound quite different from when it's full. Furthermore, there's little you can tell from the stage about how the balance sounds out in the hall. And, indeed, the balance may vary in different parts of the hall.

DALLEY   We play in over a hundred halls a year, and each of these has its own acoustical characteristics. If we were to start doctoring up the mu-

sic, changing lengths, dynamics, and articulations according to our impression of a hall—which can, in any case, be deceptive—it would be a
never-ending thing, and terribly disruptive.

STEINHARDT   You can drive yourself crazy with all the idiosyncrasies. In
general we find it dangerous to "play halls." You might, for instance, be
tempted to compensate for a dry hall by pushing your playing to the
edge and finally forcing the sound. All this isn't to say that the variants
from hall to hall might not affect our performances very slightly. In a
dry hall we may tend, almost unconsciously, to hold notes a shade
longer, and in a resonant hall, to articulate with extra care. But that's a
subtle, instinctive process, not a planned happening.

SOYER   Basically speaking, if a hall is good, it's good, and if it's bad, it's
bad. You can't make it better by playing softer, louder, slower, or faster.
You have to play what you hear yourself and make your own balance on
stage; beyond that, there's little you can do. When they asked Belmonte
what he did to train for a bullfight, he responded, "What do you want
me to do? I weigh a hundred and thirty-five pounds; a bull weighs
eleven hundred. I smoke cigars and pray a lot."

DALLEY   One encouraging trend we've noted over the twenty years
we've performed together is that a growing number of people are beginning to recognize that chamber music need not be relegated to small
halls. It used to be assumed as a matter of course that large halls are
unsuitable for string-quartet music. We don't accept that view. There are
a few nearly ideal halls where everyone can hear and see well, but they're
not necessarily small halls; the Philharmonie in Berlin would be an example. Carnegie Hall is much better suited for string quartets than many
small halls we have played in, some of which have lifeless acoustics.

STEINHARDT   The inconsistencies have always struck us as being odd.
Nobody thinks twice about going to Carnegie Hall to hear a solo violinist or a Lieder recital, where every word has to be understood; yet many
would scoff at the idea of presenting a string quartet there.

TREE   It all comes back to a widespread basic misunderstanding about
chamber music. Quartet playing is often thought of in terms of
"house music," implying a congenial gathering: good friends, good food,
and good music. That's all very well, and I must confess that my first
exposure to quartet playing was under such circumstances. Let's not
forget, however, that during the time when the bulk of this music was
written, from Haydn onwards, most instrumental music, whether it be

quartets or symphonies, was played in halls of the same size. Certainly from the artistic point of view, the emotions expressed in the great chamber-music repertoire are sometimes enough to blow the roof off of any hall. We hope that our approach to quartet playing will help dispel the image of chamber music as being something rather precious and elitist. The very term "chamber music" is a misnomer; I'd like to see it done away with. Ensemble music, yes; string-quartet music, yes. Nobody will be able to convince me that such pieces as the last quartets of Beethoven or Schubert should be looked upon as small-scale works, whether in conception, execution, or the setting in which they're to be performed.

What's your approach to learning a new piece? Do you study the score in advance?

SOYER We'll bring a score to rehearsals for reference. But our tendency is to begin to know and understand the work as we play it. Then if there are things that are unclear, we'll consult the score.

Wilhelm Furtwängler wrote, "The widely held view that the more rehearsals, the better, is a mistaken one."★ He believed that the performance should not be robbed of an element of improvisation.

DALLEY We would surely agree. We've noticed that when we've over-rehearsed a piece, the general tone of the performance will begin to deteriorate. Preserving a sense of spontaneity is of crucial importance to a group that has to play, as we do, many works forty times or more within a single season. Just for our own survival—not to mention the interest and appreciation of the public—we have to allow a degree of improvisation into our performances.

When you rehearse a piece that you've played before, what do you normally give attention to?

STEINHARDT If we haven't played a certain quartet for a year, we'll go through it carefully, looking at difficult spots and assimilating any new ideas that come to mind. Once everything is in its proper place—the notes are there, intonation problems are dealt with, our signals are set as far as leading is concerned—then we feel that a lot has to be left to the moment. We'll walk out on stage and just go with the music. And

★ Wilhelm Furtwängler, *Concerning Music* (London: Boosey & Hawkes, 1953).

each one of us will be aware that he himself or one of the others may go a little crazy and do something he's never done before.

DALLEY   Perish the thought!

TREE   I hope it doesn't appear too pretentious if I characterize what we do by referring to Tolstoy. In *War and Peace* he satirizes the Prussian school of military strategy and maintains that, contrary to popular belief, the course of events is determined not by the decisions of great leaders but by an endless chain of small, individual acts. He describes a regiment that's about to face defeat when, suddenly, a young soldier seizes the fallen flag and, rushing towards the enemy, inspires a thousand men to follow him; a single, unexpected, spontaneous act can turn the tide of the battle. Now, the playing of quartet music is, after all, an organic process. Each of us is influenced by constantly fluctuating circumstances. Every moment of our playing is conditioned by what has just occurred or by what we think is about to occur. It remains creative because just about anything can happen.

Particularly on those occasions when the violist seizes the flag!

TREE   Of course; that's what makes it fun.

SOYER   That's what quartet playing is all about. The whole business is reactive; that's the key to spontaneity. People who know us only from recordings may say that the Guarneri Quartet plays a given piece in a particular way. But it should be kept in mind that a recording only preserves a performance of a work on a certain day at a certain time. Two days or a week later it may not be just the same; years later it may be very different indeed.

Do you enjoy recording?

DALLEY   No.

TREE   No.

SOYER   No.

STEINHARDT   *Absolutely* no.

Why don't you enjoy it? Please try to be more explicit!

SOYER   It's a sterile situation; the setting is antimusical. There's no audience; you're playing to a battery of microphones. The process is corrupting. You play a piece many times; the mikes aren't right, the balance isn't right, there may be mistakes, you're unhappy with something. And as you make takes of a movement over and over again, your perceptions begin to alter. What you would have at first considered a good tempo may seem too slow because you've heard it so many times. So on the finished version we may end up doing something that's glib—because it's take number ten.

STEINHARDT   Glenn Gould had just the opposite reaction—one which we don't share. He said, "What I don't like about public performance is the non-take-twoness of it."

SOYER   For us, the very take-oneness of it is what makes public performance exciting and challenging, and generally more interesting and compelling than recorded performance. There's a tendency to want to play it safe when recording and be doubly sure of note-perfection. This can have a deadening effect.

TREE   If people were willing to listen to records as they do live performances, they would forgive minor blemishes. The whole thing is a question of attitude as to what one will or won't accept.

DALLEY   I think that the players themselves are to blame for this attitude, which gives the highest priority to perfection.

TREE   Well, let's try putting out records that have blemishes, and see what the critics and public have to say.

DALLEY   In the era of the 78s, when splices couldn't be made, the public accepted the situation and bought the record appreciating the similarity to concert conditions. Even in the age of the LP, some of the most famous recordings are of live performances.

Furtwängler, Lipatti, Toscanini . . . and many others.

DALLEY   Maybe half the recordings of jazz are taken from live performance, aren't they?

SOYER   That's the nature of jazz, isn't it? Spontaneity is the important thing.

STEINHARDT   But the nature of classical music is also spontaneity. Spontaneity with order—or however you might want to put it.

SOYER   Casals had a wonderful attitude. When recording a piece, he would play it once, and the producer might ask, "*Maître,* would you play that again? There was a note out of tune." And Casals would say, "Yes, that's right; that's the way I happened to play it." The only way you could get him to do it over again was to say that the machinery had broken down. Casals's recording of the Dvořák Concerto with Szell was played *once*. It was truly a performance; he played it and went home.

TREE   The same was true of his recording of the Schumann Concerto— it has a tremendous intensity.

A couple of years ago I recorded the two Brahms viola sonatas with Richard Goode. We made a pact to do this without any splices, and we were as nervous as if it had been before a live performance. We played each sonata through twice in its entirety, letting the chips fall where they may.

SOYER   I think it's fair to say that we don't take as much time to record as we used to. If the overall expression is there as we believe it should be, we'll allow a few things to go through which we might not have accepted in the past.

STEINHARDT   It's not as if we've improved as a quartet in terms of ensemble or intonation . . .

SOYER   But we have different priorities; that's what it really is.

TREE   I don't listen to our records, but maybe they're not as clean these days as they used to be.

DALLEY   I dust them every day.

When the Guarneri Quartet was formed, you received warm encouragement from members of the Budapest Quartet. Do you think that, to some extent, you carry on their tradition?

DALLEY   I would say that every quartet of the present day owes something to the Budapest. We admire many aspects of their playing: their warmth, their vitality. While we don't always agree with their ideas on interpretation, we greatly appreciate their wonderful sense of style, their aristocratic elegance. Their playing had a sheen to it. Our playing, by comparison, is not always so polished. For example, their recording of the *Grosse Fuge* is very different in conception from ours.

SOYER   There's one way in which we have carried on the Budapest Quartet's tradition. I'm referring to the concert when they had to stop playing because Sasha Schneider discovered that the last page of his part for a Brahms quartet was missing.

TREE I suspect that we're coming to the "letter L" incident.

DALLEY That was a high point in the history of the Guarneri Quartet.

TREE Let me explain. We were performing Beethoven's Opus 59, No. 3 in New York. Suddenly, while playing the Minuet, I realized that I didn't have the first page of the Finale before me—only the second page, which began at letter L. I began feverishly turning. John's eyes were glued to me; he knew that I was in desperate trouble, but there was nothing he could do to help.

DALLEY I felt terrible for him. At the same time, I thought, "This could only happen to Michael; he's so careful about having everything in proper order."

STEINHARDT So when we came to the transition to the Finale, Michael stopped and whispered, "Let's start from letter L."

TREE I thought it might be better to play part of the movement than no movement at all.

STEINHARDT And Dave said, "That's preposterous; we can't start in the middle of the movement. Tell the audience that you don't have the music." By this time the murmurings in the audience were almost deafening. And then Michael suddenly found the page and began to play with tremendous excitement.

TREE Like a wild man, totally out of control.

STEINHARDT John was hardly able to stay together with him. It took us about a third of the movement to regain our equilibrium.

TREE Not only were the pages in the wrong order, but I had slit them in the middle to accommodate page turns. That meant that I constantly had to turn half-pages back and forth. I was in a tizzy.

SOYER In the next day's *Wall Street Journal* the critic wrote, "One of the members of the quartet got lost."

DALLEY What had most terrified Michael was the thought that he might not have the music at all. The Budapest Quartet had felt so bad about not having been able to finish the work that they played it again in a free concert.

TREE In my hysteria at the moment, that story ran through my mind.

SOYER He was thinking, "My God, we may have to play without a fee!"—while John was thinking, "*He* can play a free concert, but not me."

TREE   I would have made a transcription of the Finale for viola solo. In self-defense, however, I must say that this was the only time in all our concerts that I've ever mixed up pages.

What advice did the Budapest Quartet members give you?

SOYER   Aside from some pointers about ensemble, their advice was primarily of a personal rather than a musical nature. They counselled us not to socialize together more than necessary, to retain a healthy independence, because quartet life inevitably involves innumerable receptions and dinner parties which require our being together. And the mere fact of traveling, rehearsing, performing, and recording together means that we probably spend more time in each other's company than we do with our families.

TREE   Being in a quartet is almost like being in a marriage, and in some respects it's harder than a marriage. I had played quartets off and on for many years, but I never realized just how great the sense of commitment must be on the part of every player in a permanent ensemble. As a solo artist or an orchestra member it would certainly be easier to choose not to participate in a particular tour or to cancel a concert in the middle of a tour if one isn't feeling well. As a member of a quartet you come to realize that you're responsible for other people's reputations and livelihoods as well as your own. One begins to feel a deep personal commitment offstage as well as on.

Have there been times when this commitment has been put to the test?

DALLEY   On quite a few occasions one of us, when struck by illness, would surely have preferred to stay home and not play. It's very rare for any of us to have to miss an engagement. When that's happened, we've either appeared as a string trio or engaged a pianist at the last moment to play piano quartets.

STEINHARDT   We've played well over two thousand concerts together and have missed no more than seven or eight for reasons of health; so I think we have a pretty good batting average. But we have to keep in shape; that means pacing ourselves rather carefully when on tour.

TREE   Even some of our activities apart from the quartet are governed by our sense of commitment to one another. For instance, one or two of us once expressed an interest in taking a ski break in the middle of a European tour. The matter was discussed and voted down because it was considered just a bit too risky and not very conducive to everyone's peace of mind. We do, however, take a prolonged summer vacation, and then the Guarneri String Quartet ceases to exist for a time—thank God!—and what each of us does is nobody's business but his own.

THE SHAPING
PROCESS

Tuning; Intonation

Let's now turn to various aspects of quartet playing and look at them in some detail. Putting first things first: Does the quartet follow a regular procedure when tuning?

SOYER   Yes. We have Michael give us the A. This originated from the fact that he's always played on steel strings with synthetic core, which don't readily go out of tune, while we others have sometimes played on strings with gut core, which are more easily affected by climate. As Michael was the most consistently accurate, we've retained the habit of relying on him. We'll even refer to his A if we have to tune onstage in the middle of a concert.

DALLEY   We'll first tune carefully offstage, but when we go from the green room to the stage, we often find that the temperature and degree of humidity are quite different, and our careful tuning has been for nought. Of course, when we find it necessary to tune between movements we try to do so quickly and discreetly, so as not to break the mood and distract the public.

STEINHARDT   We try to keep out of each other's way. If someone is having a bit of trouble with a string, the others will stop. And so, keeping a low profile, we each tune separately. On rare occasions one of us may indicate to another that a certain string needs correction. Someone will whisper, "My A is not your A."

The concept of tuning separately is extremely valuable. I'm reminded of the practice of Sir Henry Wood three-quarters of a century ago, but seldom followed since, when every single member of the Queen's Hall Orchestra had to pass

before him and his tuning device to test his A—which in those days was set at
435.4 vibrations per second. To what pitch does the Quartet tune?

TREE Basically to 440. I sometimes tune just a mite above the tuning
fork, but not nearly so high as pianos are normally tuned. I think that
stringed instruments are happier when the pitch isn't too high. We're
very conservative along those lines. Nowadays one often hears, especially in Europe, the A tuned up to 444 or 445, and that makes a hell of
a difference!

In addition to the general tuning, there will be specific tunings called
for. The viola and cello sometimes have to play their open C strings
together in the course of a movement. There are a few crucial places.
For example, in the first movement of Beethoven's Opus 59, No. 1—

—I find that if I don't tune my C string to match perfectly with the
cello's before the piece begins, there's a major risk of that octave sounding out of tune. To remind myself, I scrawl at the top of the music,
"Check C with Dave!"

SOYER Another important consideration in tuning is that, as Casals
pointed out, the two lower strings of the cello—and of the viola, too—
should be tuned just a shade sharp. In other words, the G string is
brought up a little, narrowing the fifth between the G and D; the C is
then raised accordingly. This creates much better intonation when playing with the violins or with a piano.

TREE We often begin concerts with Beethoven's Opus 18, No. 1. In the
very second bar everyone plays a C natural [see page 60], but the viola
is the only instrument using the open string. Do you know that even
with my C string tuned higher, I must have my first finger ready to
place on the string just above the nut, because if I play the open C at
normal volume it tends to sound flat in comparison with the violins?
Don't ask me why. It could be that at the beginning of a concert, if
someone is the slightest bit on edge, the intonation may tend to rise.

DALLEY   High-register instruments seem to have an inclination to creep up in pitch. I've noticed this innumerable times.

TREE   Even on the viola, I find that if there's a long legato line that has open strings within it, I have to concentrate on keeping the pitch down. I often tell my students to take a long view of a passage. If an open string is about to occur, keep the intonation within reason, because the open string won't adjust.

String players are fortunate in having considerable latitude in intonation beyond the fixed, equal-tempered tuning of the piano. Depending on its context, a D sharp may be quite different from an E flat. To what extent do you use "expressive intonation," as Casals called it, in quartet playing?

STEINHARDT   The difficulty in string-quartet intonation is to determine the degree of freedom you have at any given moment. Two factors come into play: the linear and the vertical. By "linear" I'm referring to the sense of melodic or harmonic direction in the individual line; semitones in particular have a tendency to be drawn slightly up or down as the case may be. In this sense "expressive intonation" is an essential element of interpretation. The other factor—the vertical—is the necessity to be in tune with your colleagues, to hear your individual note in relation to the chord being played at that moment. Both factors are important and demand a highly responsive ear and instant adaptability.

Among the "vertical" considerations there are anchor points: these are octaves, fourths, and fifths. When played simultaneously these intervals should be exact [i.e., played with pure (or just) rather than equal-tempered intonation]. I make mental notes as to where they occur. I'll know that in bar 9 of a certain movement I play a B above the viola's F sharp, and this therefore leaves me virtually no leeway for subjectivity in intonation. I say "virtually" because every rule can have an exception: a problem may arise, for instance, if I want my B to lead to a C that follows. Should I play the B high? That's a hard choice to make and shows how the linear and vertical demands sometimes conflict. On the other hand, seconds, thirds, sixths, and sevenths, whether major or minor, are up for grabs, as are augmented or diminished fourths and fifths; in all these cases there's considerably more flexibility than with perfect fourths and fifths.

One could cite endless examples of expressive intonation at work. It's really a habit of playing. For instance, in the slow movement of Beethoven's Opus 18, No. 1, close semitones—in this case drawn upwards—increase the sense of expressive tension:

Adagio affettuoso ed appassionato

Such passages would lose their eloquence if played with equal-tempered intonation.

TREE   Or take the following passage from the second movement of Beethoven's Opus 59, No. 3:

Andante con moto quasi Allegretto

Beethoven modulates at this point to the key of F minor; it's a poignant moment. The cello's low C's establish the dominant. My D flats (on the dominant ninth) have a downwards tendency, while the E's (leading note) have an upwards tendency. In bar 27 the G flat (Neapolitan sixth) comes as a surprise. I would draw this note particularly downwards, thereby heightening its expressive impact and emphasizing the difference between it and the G naturals that appear elsewhere in the phrase.

STEINHARDT   There are times when the composer will indicate an enharmonic change, as Mozart does when modulating from B flat to G minor in the first movement of the G-minor Quintet [K. 516]:

The F sharp in bar 93 should be drawn ever so slightly higher than the G flat in the previous bar. One could change the fingering for the F sharp, or even the string on which it's played. Beethoven has a similar enharmonic change at the transition to the development of the first movement of Opus 59, No. 2 [see page 93].

Would the chromatic transition passage in the Finale of Mozart's G-major Quartet [K. 387] be another example of close semitone relationships?

TREE   Yes. We would raise the sharpened notes slightly, but in this case we have to be a little careful because the motif is repeated many times, and if the intonation is exaggerated it may tend to sound increasingly so with the repetitions. We definitely believe in expressive intonation, but it has to be treated with care. We've heard playbacks of our performances that have alerted us to the danger of going too far. However, I'd sooner err in that direction than play with a sterile and static equaltempered intonation.

DALLEY   The chorale in the Lydian mode from Beethoven's Opus 132 [see page 38] would be a case where the intonation shouldn't be overly rich in implication but as neutral as possible: with no exaggerated leading notes, and fourths and fifths that are as pure as can be, allowing the overtones to mingle with the least possible clash.

The exact kind of intonation used sometimes varies many times within the course of a movement, depending on the musical context. However, I don't want to give the impression that the differences are huge; they are sometimes almost imperceptible. That's why an artist such as Milstein, who plays with expressive intonation, can perform beautifully with a piano, making the adaptation in unison passages when required. A player of that caliber can alter his sense of intonation at the given moment. That sort of flexibility is what everyone should strive for. Even if you have a good ear, it should never be taken for granted; it must always be kept alert and developed.

Since you're often playing a middle voice, John, are there times when you have to adjust a repeated note in different directions?

DALLEY   Absolutely. Look, for example, at the following passage from the slow movement of Beethoven's Opus 132:

Molto adagio

I have six successive middle C's. The other players should be aware of this and, in principle, adjust to me, as these are relatively ironclad notes. But at the moment of performance I'll have to be ready, if necessary, to adjust to any fluctuations going on around me.

SOYER   The cellist has a special concern in that the others' notes must often adjust to the harmonic implication of the bass. When I first began to play quartets I wondered how to treat a line in the bass that while primarily harmonic in nature also has its own sense of melodic direction. For instance, if I have the notes E–G sharp–A, should I play the G sharp high, even though it's in the bass? I've concluded that the bass does indeed have a life of its own—even if there are times when I can't shape my intonation in an extreme way. The coda of the first movement of Beethoven's Opus 59, No. 2 provides an interesting example:

I think of these notes in a linear fashion, almost as if the bass line were a melody. The passage begins in the key of G-sharp minor; the G natural in bar 215 is clearly a simplified way of writing F double-sharp, which, as the leading note, has an upwards attraction towards the tonic G sharp. For this reason I'd avoid using the open G string and would play the passage on the C string. When G natural comes again [bar 223], its harmonic function is altered; it's now the fifth degree of C major and thus *not* sharpened. The subsequent G sharp [bar 224] is no longer the tonic but acts as the leading note in A minor and *should* be sharpened. This is the explanation from the harmonic standpoint, but your hearing, once sensitized to such things, will often be able to put you there quite of itself without your needing to think it out.

John touched on a certain problem area when he referred to unison playing. When four string players have passages in unison, the question is always who is to adjust to whom—especially when expressive intonation is involved. Take the second movement of Beethoven's Opus 132:

Close semitones are called for here, but if someone exaggerates, it can throw things out of kilter. There has to be discretion.

TREE   Sometimes when rehearsing unison passages we may use commonplace expressions like "Let's hit the note on the head." Then if we find that our intonation is better matched, one of us may say, "But don't you find that it's a bit sexless? This particular note has a yearning quality." As Dave says, the problem lies in coming to an agreement as to *how much* the note strives upwards or downwards.

DALLEY   Open strings can be a problem when it comes to expressive intonation. It depends on what key you're in. If you're in D or A, where the open strings sound the tonic or dominant, there's no difficulty. But an open A string in F major, where it is the third degree of the scale, may tend to sound slightly flat. You can either adjust the intonation by placing your finger just above the nut or avoid the open string. Many players think that open strings should be constant and everything else should adapt accordingly. But in a practical sense that's untrue. If you're sitting there with that open string which is supposed to be a major third in F major, you're out of luck.

STEINHARDT   You sometimes find situations where an instrument may have preceded you in establishing a certain pitch—perhaps at a lower octave—and even if you think that you could improve on the other player's intonation, you still have to adjust to what you hear at that moment; you have to go with your colleague for better or worse. Then, after the concert, you can grab him by the tie and say, "How dare you play that way!"

DALLEY   In performance there is a great deal of fluctuation of intonation that the listener's ear doesn't pick up, because everything is heard in relativity to the given moment. One hears a certain chord that is in tune with itself and the ear is satisfied. A few bars later the same chord may come again, and so long as it is again in tune with itself, the ear finds no fault with it, even though, strictly speaking, the pitch may not be absolutely identical to what was heard earlier. Obviously, such changes—if they occur at all—are very subtle. I mention them only to emphasize that intonation is something infinitely flexible and not a fixed entity.

Do you find that young musicians normally need a great deal of training to become sensitized to expressive intonation?

SOYER   Only when they've been playing for a long time without having had exposure to it. If they have been taught to listen that way early in their studies, it becomes second nature.

How do you rehearse intonation in the quartet?

STEINHARDT   By playing softly, slowly, and, if necessary, in combinations to be able to isolate the problem. Say it's a unison passage, and after a couple of repetitions it doesn't get any better. Then the cello and viola may work on it together, and they'll ask each other if this note can be played higher, or that one lower. John and I will listen and be their critics, and then they will act as our critics. Hopefully things will be cleared up.

What effect does balance have on intonation? Are there times when a note will sound more in tune if it's played louder or softer in the overall texture?

DALLEY   In general, intonation in octave passages is helped considerably when the upper voice plays a little more lightly than the others. This may be because the upper voice reinforces the first overtone of the lower voice. The same thing is true when you play octaves on your own; the sound is better when the lower note is the stronger of the two. Young groups are startled at how much better octaves can sound when balanced in this way.

STEINHARDT   Balance could also be a factor in various harmonic situations. Say that in an E-major triad you are playing a G sharp—the third degree—rather high. Played too loudly, that G sharp might tend to chafe, to sound eccentric; but played softly, it will take its natural place in the chord and give a nice character to it.

SOYER   It should be remembered, too, that trills need special consideration when it comes to intonation. When a finger touches the fingerboard quickly, it tends not to go all the way down; nor do you have time to place the whole pad of the fingertip on the string. Consequently, if you trill with customary intonation, the upper note will sound flat. To compensate, you should play the upper note of the trill a little sharp; then it sounds on pitch.

Vibrato

Time and again I've had the experience of hearing string players whose general level of accomplishment is very high but whose vibrato, even if attractive, remains relatively undeveloped in the sense that it's monotonous or subject to mannerism. On the other hand, nothing is more beautiful than a vibrato shaped with artistic sensitivity. May I have your thoughts on the subject of vibrato in general and its use in quartet playing?

DALLEY   It's hard to define the essence of a vibrato. Of all aspects of string playing it's the most difficult to analyze or teach. To a large extent one's vibrato develops of itself and becomes second nature, just like one's way of bowing or of holding the instrument. I think that if you were to analyze the tone of famous string players you would find a close relationship between the qualities and attributes of their vibratos and their personalities—the intensity of a Heifetz, the comparative relaxation of a Kreisler. I'd even go so far as to say that in many cases there's something of a relationship between one's tone and one's own speaking voice. This is just a personal, not a scientific, observation.

STEINHARDT   It's interesting to note from recordings of Thibaud and Casals made well over a half-century ago that, though there was a great deal of freedom as far as rubato was concerned, vibrato was used with far more refinement and discretion than one normally finds today. The same is true of the vocal tradition. Great singers of the early part of the century whom we know from recordings had fine, pure vibratos. I think there is nowadays, generally speaking, a decline of taste in the use of vibrato. While the precise quality of a string player's vibrato will always retain an indefinable personal element, a certain amount can nonetheless be taught and understood about its usage.

DALLEY   Which is the master and which the servant: the vibrato or the player? Generally speaking, there are two main problems: inequality in the production of vibrato (owing to technical limitations) and lack of variety in its application.

SOYER   Taking the first of these problems, there's a tendency to emphasize the vibrato on certain notes just because they lie conveniently under the hand. This comes from not listening carefully enough to what one does.

TREE   Sometimes I'll play for students exactly what they've played for me, and they'll cringe because they'll hear dead notes coming out of an otherwise lovely phrase. And these are players with good vibratos. The fourth finger, for instance, is often neglected, and, strangely enough, the first finger as well, especially when it acts as the pivotal point before a shift. Sometimes you may be so preoccupied with the shift that's going to take place that you're thinking one or two notes ahead, and the vibrato stops.

Sándor Végh, first violinist of the Végh Quartet, stresses that the vibrato should be part of the shift. The vibrato already puts the hand in motion, and that motion carries into the shift. He sometimes speaks of "the legato of the left hand."

TREE   That's very well put. I agree that if used correctly, the vibrato serves to keep the hand supple and relaxed. It's a bit like a lubricant on each note.

SOYER   One of the most annoying mannerisms is the habit of starting the vibrato only after the note has begun.

TREE   That's wonderful for blues singers.

Vibrato is often neglected, particularly by amateur players, on short, detached notes in quiet accompaniment figures.

DALLEY By professionals as well. One shouldn't forget that a short note doesn't have much time to come to life. Not only vibrato but vital left-hand articulation becomes increasingly important in setting the string in vibration. This applies as well to a quick note in a legato passage. In the second subject from the first movement of Schubert's "Death and the Maiden" Quartet, if the left hand fails to articulate the sixteenth notes, the ear simply doesn't pick them up.

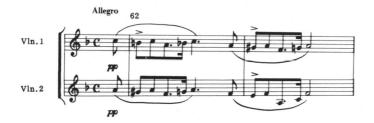

In such cases Alexander Schneider used to say, "Even if you're playing piano with the right hand, play fortissimo with the left hand."

TREE When students pass over short notes as if they're inconsequential, I ask them to imagine that the phrase they're playing is being sung and that the notes have words attached to them. Just as a singer will enunciate each syllable, every one of those notes needs vibrato and articulation.

Perhaps we could consider now the second aspect John mentioned: the need for variety in vibrato.

STEINHARDT Once the vibrato is brought under technical control the real challenge begins. Even the most gorgeous vibrato can become monotonous if it is not used creatively. Some young players who think they have finished their studies may find that disconcerting, but there are laws of expression, and you just have to try to live by them. The ability to widen or narrow the vibrato, to alter its speed, and to make such a change even in the course of a single note gives life and character to interpretation.

TREE Teachers don't sufficiently stress that vibrato is a musical device—a tool that should constantly be adjusted to the demands of the music, and not just poured over everything like maple syrup over a stack of hotcakes.

SOYER   The maple-syrup vibrato becomes meaningless—like someone going around smiling constantly no matter what he says. It would be just as well to have no vibrato as always to vibrate in the same way. Casals's recordings reveal how meaningful vibrato can be. For instance, in the adagio introduction to the Finale of Beethoven's A-major Cello Sonata [Opus 69] the theme is first stated by the piano, the cello taking the accompaniment. Casals plays almost without vibrato—first of all because he doesn't have the melody, and second because it would sound silly to have the accompanying voice playing with an intense vibrato under the nonvibrato of the piano. And then when the cello takes the melody, Casals adds just a touch of vibrato, and it's as if the sun comes out.

DALLEY   That sort of contrast and variety in the use of vibrato can be applied to countless passages in the quartet literature. Take the "Heiliger Dankgesang" from Beethoven's Opus 132. In the opening statement we differentiate the quarter-note figure from the chorale, which moves in half notes, the quarter-note figure being played with vibrato—albeit very refined—and the chorale beginning with no vibrato at all. We then gradually add vibrato as the crescendo develops. We continue this pattern throughout the whole first section.

The Molto adagio returns twice in the course of the movement, the opening figure each time taking on a more elaborate rhythmic motion.

We reflect this growing agitation by a progressive increase in vibrato. There's an evolution of intensity, but it's an inner intensity, as if one were whispering something very important.

I've been struck by the nuances of vibrato in your performance of the slow movement of Beethoven's Opus 74. Would you comment on this?

STEINHARDT The opening theme is a beautiful, heartfelt song:

It's a direct expression and should be silvery and appealing. It needs a lovely but unexaggerated vibrato; anything in excess would spoil the theme's inherent simplicity.

Midway through the movement there's that wonderful passage in D flat:

Since the piano in the preceding bar is followed by a diminuendo, we begin bar 87 pianissimo. The music takes on a special intimacy; it's a deeply touching moment. I thin down the vibrato but nonetheless maintain a certain intensity. We grade the degree of vibrato from the first violin downwards. The first violin gives just a little—an inward tenderness; the viola gives less; and the cello none at all. The completely tranquil bass allows the first violin liberty to speak without exaggeration.

DALLEY   At bar 103 Beethoven suddenly modulates to A-flat minor and writes a subito *pp;* five bars later "espressivo" is indicated.

At the *pp* we eliminate the vibrato entirely and barely touch the string with the bow; the change to A-flat minor thereby takes on a hushed, almost ominous quality. At the "espressivo" we give a little more substance to the sound under the bow and add warmth of vibrato. We think this provides the contrast in color that Beethoven had in mind.

SOYER   Sometimes playing without vibrato can create a kind of intensity of its own, as in the *pp* introduction to Beethoven's Opus 132. Played in this way the notes convey a mysterious sense of foreboding.

The line is preserved by very legato string crossings, expressive intonation, and the alla breve motion. The vibrato is reserved for the "hairpins," and their effect is therefore all the more arresting.

STEINHARDT   Szigeti would sometimes purposely withhold vibrato from a single note; he magnified the expression by, as it were, cooling it off. This was highly unusual and very personal.

DALLEY   The main point to remember is that all nuances have to be thought of not only in terms of volume but of intensity. You may, for instance, want to add intensity to the sound without making a crescendo, and that can be done by the left hand. A minute increase in vibrato can bring a moment of unexpected life.

SOYER   By the same token, a decrease in vibrato can bring a sense of repose. One sometimes hears a player making a diminuendo to pianissimo on the final note of a phrase, with the bow becoming lighter and lighter, yet the left-hand intensity remains unchanged; there's no feeling of tranquillity. At such times my teacher Diran Alexanian would say, "That sounds like someone playing fortissimo at a great distance."

There's much debate as to whether vibrato should emanate from the arm, wrist, or finger.

DALLEY   If I had to break it down in detail, I'd say that the greater part of the violin vibrato comes from the knuckles, a somewhat lesser part from the wrist, and the remainder from the forearm. But the main point is that *everything* is in motion: the movement emanates from the forearm and flows down through the knuckles, which react like supple hinges. Even the violin itself—if not held too tightly—moves ever so slightly in response to the vibrato.

STEINHARDT   Many students tighten their grip when they play. They may get away with it in a fashion, because a young person's body is limber, but as time goes on this can lead to serious difficulties. It's incumbent on a young professional to learn how to vibrate in the most natural way possible. I played with an arm vibrato for many years, my first teachers having tried in vain to teach me a wrist vibrato. However, as I felt I was expending too much energy, I gradually managed to develop a wrist vibrato as well, which gave me more variety and greater relaxation. But, as John has said, the real motion of vibrato is transferred through the joints of the finger, and these must be supple and yielding.

TREE   Speaking as a violinist who came late to the viola, I've learned from experience that one can't vibrate with the same width and speed on the larger instrument as on the smaller. Otherwise a nanny-goat effect may be the result. That's almost inevitable at first. But as one gets used to the viola, one will begin instinctively to incorporate more arm movement, to widen the vibrato and to slow it down a little.

SOYER   The cellist's basic vibrato comes mainly from the arm, with, of course, flexibility of the wrist and finger. Naturally there's much variation, depending on the specific nature of the music. However, in general, the vibrato on the cello is wider than on the other instruments and becomes yet wider and somewhat slower as one progresses into the lower register. The heavy, ropelike C string doesn't respond to fast oscillation as readily as the thinner A string. If you play a note in first position on the A string and then place the same finger in first position on the C string using the same vibrato, you'll find that the lower note vibrates too rapidly; you'll have a nanny goat in basso profondo.

TREE   After giving due attention to the intrinsic differences between the instruments, I'd say that every one of us constantly looks for variety in coloration and will experiment with every type of vibrato. Even on the viola I'll use a finger vibrato if I want it to be fast and narrow, producing an intense, glistening sound. But I'll use more wrist, and eventually more arm, if I want to find a fatter, more sensuous quality, particularly on a lower string. Take one of the favorite works of all quartet players: Smetana's *From My Life*. The opening celebrates the vigor and enthusiasm of a young man seeing the world as if for the first time [see page 78]. It's very declamatory, and certainly the vibrato wants to be highly intense and full of ardor. In the same movement there are moments that are much more quiet and tender. And the slow movement is absolutely heartbreaking—it's so poignant, so beautiful. It would be almost a crime to vibrate in the same fashion as at the beginning of the piece.

I'm a little leery of the manuals which stress exclusively the physical means by which vibrato can be produced. Vibrato has to come from the imagination as well. If you imagine a certain color, you'll find that color. But if you can't imagine it, it won't come, even if you have the technical means at your disposal.

STEINHARDT   Yes, it's true. Some players do things very awkwardly, but they succeed in bringing out the music. Of course, it's better not to do things awkwardly; nonetheless, the power of the imagination is something marvelous.

DALLEY   Nothing of real beauty can be produced without it.

More on the Left Hand;
Hints on Practicing

Another aspect of coloration is the use of harmonics. I enjoy a harmonic from time to time when it momentarily lightens a texture, but I find the habit of using harmonics on long expressive notes in the middle of a melody to be most disconcerting.

STEINHARDT   If George Szell were here he would hug you. In his grave he is smiling! That was one of his favorite subjects. His chief complaint was about cellists. Not that we violinists are free from blame in this respect, but cellists rely upon harmonics as a crutch more than we do. I myself use harmonics very rarely, sometimes for special effects—say, when the last note of a phrase in the high register should have a simplicity and purity, and you're slowing down the vibrato in any case. But the exceptions prove the rule.

SOYER   Cellists have a special problem in that their strings are more than double the length of those of the violin. Harmonics—especially the one that's halfway up the A string—are useful in helping one to move to and from the higher positions. The problem is that their use becomes habitual, and one finds oneself applying them to melodic notes more as a convenience than as a means of expression. Harmonics that don't fit into the context of the phrase shouldn't be used. I limit their use mostly to scales and rapid passage work, where they're not noticed.

Do you also use open strings as a natural aid to scale playing?

SOYER   I definitely do.

DALLEY   It's odd, but people usually teach scales without open strings. I don't know why that should be. Perhaps they think it simplifies matters too much. Naturally, one should be able to do both. But certainly in a very pragmatic sense you need the open strings.

STEINHARDT   I'm a great believer in the first position and the use of open strings wherever they're appropriate.

TREE   As a general principle, playing in lower positions can help towards a clearer and cleaner sound throughout the whole quartet. Now, of course, there are many exceptions to this, and I'm the first to enjoy shifting into higher positions for the sake of a warmer or meatier sound. But one has to watch very carefully that one is free to do that at the given moment—that the overall timbre of the group doesn't suffer, doesn't become covered or muffled.

DALLEY   There are three main reasons for using open strings: for ease, for clarity, and for emphasis when needed. They're also useful when you have melodic figures that cross strings and you want the groupings of notes to fall in a logical progression.

Many times in Mozart you have rapid passages under long legato bows, in which every note should be crystalline, just as the notes should sound on the piano in one of the concertos. And you often have difficulties in fingering these passages. Playing in the first position and using open strings then brings both ease and clarity. I know that Michael will sometimes go far out of his way to cross strings with the bow to enable the left hand to stay in the low positions.

May we have an example, please?

TREE   Take the Trio from the Scherzo of Beethoven's Opus 74. There are sixteen bars—all in C major—where the viola plays the theme in octaves with the cello. One wants as much clarity and brilliance as possible.

Rather than play in the third position or simply use the fourth finger in first position, I use open strings wherever feasible. There are at least six times when this requires an extra string crossing, and at one point [bar 149] I cross over two strings for just one note. What I do may look like the devil. One's right arm may feel as if it's falling off, especially in the quasi prestissimo tempo. One has to have the arm ready and cocked so that with a flick of the wrist it extends over two strings and then comes immediately back again. I would never consent to such a fingering if I didn't know how well it makes the passage sound. It's not what teachers would normally advise their students to do.

SOYER   Many cellists have a complex about open strings. Students are often told, "Never play an open string if you can avoid it." Well, I once had the opportunity of playing a Bach suite for Enesco, and he said, "I would suggest that you play a great deal more in the first position and use open strings much more often. This music should sound as vibrant and free as possible." He wanted to avoid anything that was stuffy, convoluted, or tricky.

DALLEY   Zimbalist told me just the same thing: "Why not use a simpler fingering? Bach wouldn't have used a fingering like that; he probably never would have thought of it. It doesn't make any sense."

SOYER   As a youngster I sometimes played in the NBC Symphony. One day, while waiting for a rehearsal to begin, I ran through about seven concertos in fifteen minutes. Frank Miller, the orchestra's solo cellist, looked at me quizzically and asked, "David, what are you doing?" "Well, Frank," I replied, "I'm warming up." "But what are you doing way up there in the high positions? You know, David, I make all my money in the first position." Casals, of course, made frequent use of open strings. He liked a clear, open sonority.

His vibrato had a purity which enabled him to pass from an open string to a stopped note without change of color.

STEINHARDT   Exactly! One has to be very careful about what surrounds an open string. In the theme of the variation movement of Beethoven's Opus 18, No. 5—

—I'll usually play the upbeat with an open A. But on the repeat, for the sake of variety I'll play the upbeat on the D string, where it has a more veiled quality. The vibrato on the F sharp will vary accordingly. The first time it will be narrow and slow to match the open A; the second time it will be linked with the vibrato of the upbeat.

We can't go into great detail about fingerings here, but are there any basic ideas you would like to put forward?

DALLEY   I always urge young players to develop a creative approach to the whole question of shifting. If one looks at the fingerings notated in the violin parts of the older German chamber-music editions still popularly used, one finds a nearly total lack of second position. There's no credible reason why an entire set of parts should be fingered minus the second position. It has to do with the way people are taught. Szigeti used to talk about playing in between the first and second positions and treating them as *one* position by means of extensions. And he would do the same with the second and third positions—finding a kind of middle ground. And Casals made one of his great contributions to cello playing by giving the hand the suppleness to play between the positions.

SOYER   He also showed the value of shifting on semitones, where the shifts are heard the least.

STEINHARDT   Sometimes, of course, one wants to hear a glissando. I think of our quartet as being rather old-fashioned, not only in regard to the extent to which we slide but in the kind of slides we use.

There's a tendency nowadays—a "purity" which goes together with the mechanical spirit of our age—to abjure glissandos. A young cellist recently told me that Mr. So-and-So plays "cleanly" because he avoids glissandos. I asked him whether the performance of a singer making a glissando in a Mozart or Verdi aria would therefore be considered "dirty."

TREE   For me, "clean" playing is a little sterile. We'll often use a glissando, not as a gimmick but as a genuine means of expression. It will come at a key place: a climax, an unexpected modulation, a change of color. We'll use it, too, at times, just for a simple leap of an interval up or down; it can be a wonderful way of connecting two notes.

STEINHARDT   It's true, though, that many students are afraid to make a glissando; they believe it may be considered in bad taste or in some way laughable. Even when they do finally hazard one, they hardly make any at all. And by the time they play the piece in a concert hall, the glissando will have all but disappeared. I often tell my students to put the instrument down and sing the passage. One quickly discovers where a glissando is natural to the life of a melody. Few of us have much vocal talent, but we do have vocal instinct.

John has said that vibrato reveals a string player's true personality—it's a mirror into his or her soul—and I think that the glissando is another part of it. Nothing in string playing is more moving than the ways in which Kreisler and Casals made glissandos. Szigeti, too, had a most expressive way of sliding, especially when, on occasion, he would drag his finger down a tone. It sounded like a cry or a lament; it was very natural, very vocal—and heart-rending.

DALLEY   There are, of course, different ways of producing glissandos. One can, for instance, slide into a note, using the finger with which the new note is to be played. Or the slide can be made by the finger playing the previous note, the new note then being dropped into place.

STEINHARDT   The second kind—favored by Kreisler as well as by Heifetz in his early days—is the one we use somewhat more often. Oddly enough, it's very instrumental, not executed in the way that would be easiest for a voice. But there's something very peaceful and loving about it. One should be careful when making a glissando not to race into a note too quickly or make an accent; that can be jarring. But I guess we use all the slides in the book.

Of course, one must be careful to avoid inadvertent glissandos through technical negligence.

SOYER   One can mask an unwelcome slide by momentarily lightening the bow pressure. That's very important, and often neglected.

STEINHARDT   On the other hand, if you want the slide to really stand out, you can bear down on it dramatically—as Heifetz did to great advantage. When it came to a searing-hot passage that culminated in a fantastic leap to a high note, he would accentuate the slide, sometimes even more than the top note. It had tremendous verve.

Would you give some examples of places where you find it natural to use a glissando?

TREE   Take the beginning of Schumann's A-major Quartet—the so-called "Clara" Quartet:

STEINHARDT   There's no way in which you could sing those lovely opening notes "cleanly"! It's a sigh. I hardly think of them as two separate notes; they're like one note.

A glissando can often be a means to bring variety or heighten the expression when a figure is repeated, as in the theme of the slow movement of Beethoven's Opus 74:

One could already make a glissando in the first phrase [(a)], but that would diminish the impact of the lovely variant in the second phrase [(b)], where the slide seems a most natural way of highlighting the C.

The middle theme in the Cavatina from Beethoven's Opus 130 is another example:

DALLEY   Yes; there again we have a repetition of a phrase. Arnold's decision as to whether or not to make a glissando from the B flat to the E flat in bar 25 depends on what I do in bar 23. If I make no glissando at all, he might make a little, or vice versa.

SOYER   I also sometimes allow myself a glissando in bar 27, when the cello takes over the expressive fall from B flat to E flat.

DALLEY   We don't plan this in advance; it's always changing. But whatever is done mustn't distort the wonderful simplicity of the passage.

STEINHARDT   A word of warning: glissandos *can* become something of a problem in a string quartet, especially when all four players feel inspired to slide at more or less the same time. Then things have to be sorted out. In general, however, a glissando is an invaluable means of expression. I feel sorry for those instrumentalists who can't make glissandos—the poor pianists!

I feel sorry for the poor string players who could make use of glissandos but don't do so.

Perhaps we could now consider some further questions relating to string technique. In rapid passages how do you deal with problems of coordination between the left hand and the bow arm?

STEINHARDT   I would normally stress the articulation of only one hand at a time. For instance, if you're playing spiccato, the fall of the bow as it bites the string does most of the articulating; the left hand should be very light. In the Paganini *Moto perpetuo* your fingers are barely touching the string. Many students clamp down their fingers at times when the bow should really be doing most of the work; it's important to know when to relax the left hand.

DALLEY   Generally, one could say that in passages of separate strokes the bow arm takes precedence, and in legato, the left hand. It's not an infallible rule, but it does often work that way. In quartet playing, the most difficult places to get together are rapid legato passages, where you don't have any articulation of the bowing to help you. In such cases good left-hand articulation is essential, not only for your own coordination but for clarity of ensemble.

SOYER   As a cellist, my point of view differs from my violinist colleagues' in that I feel that the left hand should be the guiding factor at all times—with the exception of very rapid spiccato or sautillé passages, where, yes, the bow sets up a speed and the left hand follows it. In every other instance the bow should follow the left hand.

TREE   If there's a big leap in a fast tempo, I frequently tell students to make sure that the left hand gets there before the sound speaks. That's often more difficult than the bowing.

DALLEY   There's usually a special reason for a lack of coordination: a poor fingering, a difficult string crossing, an awkward shift.

TREE   Playing a passage slowly will usually reveal the point of difficulty. A surprising number of students don't appreciate the value of slow practice. It's sometimes harder than playing quickly.

SOYER   Of course, there's also the question of *how* one practices. It's often not understood that practicing slowly is a *mental* exercise; it allows the brain to assimilate what has to be done when the passage is eventually played up to tempo. The learning process must be slow enough for comprehension to be complete and clear. A common occurrence is that a student may practice slowly but not break the problems down and understand them. Thus, after hours of work he still finds himself unable to cope with the passage when he plays it faster.

STEINHARDT   It's important when practicing slowly to approximate what you're going to do when you play rapidly. In a slow tempo you usually articulate firmly. But when playing quickly you don't press your fingers down so hard; it's more like reading braille: just touching the string. Let's say there's a difficult arpeggio passage. I'd begin by playing the shifts slowly and then increase the speed. However, from the beginning I'd try to approximate the very light finger pressure needed for the fast tempo.

DALLEY   I also recommend working on rapid passages in very short segments—playing each quickly and then stopping. Eventually the segments should be joined together. In this way the fingers learn to react quickly, but the mind need only assimilate a little at a time.

It's beneficial to one's technique to free the left hand from habitual reactions. Ivan Galamian had a systematic list of rhythms—dotted patterns or displaced accents—that could be applied to any passage. A difficult shift, for instance, would be played at various speeds, depending on the rhythmic pattern used. It's amazing how helpful it is to practice ten or twelve of these rhythms. You can concentrate without getting flurried, and your hand feels prepared for almost any eventuality. All regimens, such as scale practice, should be studied in a variety of ways to avoid routine.

STEINHARDT   I learned a lot about creative practicing from Szigeti. His mind was alive and teeming with inventive ideas. He would never just routinely practice an awkward shift to a high note over and over again; he might try shifting to a yet higher note—or in the case of a difficult fast passage, play it faster yet! Being able to do something even more difficult makes the passage itself seem easier the next time around. He was always experimenting and would often practice the same passage with different fingerings.

Do you sometimes change fingerings from one performance to another?

DALLEY   I do—a great deal. Not that I would recommend it all the time. You won't want to fool about with unison passages where the quartet has taken great care to coordinate the intonation. And when sensitive textures are involved, you won't want suddenly to play on another string just for the sake of doing something different. But otherwise it's true that you can do a lot of experimenting. I once heard Milstein play a concerto three times within a week, and I can attest to the fact that on each occasion he changed fingerings all the way through. I find that amazing; I like that kind of approach. It's vitalizing for the performer. It shouldn't divert you from the essence of the music, but it can be very creative. On the other hand, there are many fine players who rarely change their fingerings.

There are risks involved.

STEINHARDT Sometimes one should take risks. "Fingerings" as such are not essential. Every performance is unique; every time you play, you create anew. There's a sense of enjoyment, of playfulness, of spontaneity. The great pianist Josef Hofmann changed his fingering—and phrasing—so often that no two performances were alike, yet each was an organic whole.

I've noticed, Arnold, that you don't mark fingerings in your music.

STEINHARDT That's a very personal choice. Neither John nor I do.

TREE I'm the scribe of the quartet, as compared with those who prefer to see the page before them devoid of markings. But, ironically, that doesn't necessarily mean that I will follow my markings, and it certainly doesn't mean that I won't change them from concert to concert. And so my music is more filled with erasures than pencil marks. You might ask, "Why bother?" I suppose I'm something of an archivist by nature. When I take up a work again, I like to compare my present interpretation with what I've done before. For instance, this afternoon I picked up a Reger unaccompanied suite that I had worked on no more than a month ago and changed three or four very important fingerings, some pertaining to matters of color. Yet they had been written in as though they were to stay forever.

Pizzicato

DALLEY It might be worthwhile to add a word about pizzicato—something that students often take for granted but which deserves special attention. When it comes to pizzicato, the violin is at a disadvantage compared with the cello: its strings are so short that they cannot ring well.

STEINHARDT   The first violin in a quartet is particularly at a disadvantage, because its pizzicato is usually in the upper register. Rather than a musical sonority, it sounds as if a pebble fell on the floor.

DALLEY   There is, however, a certain amount one can do to help matters. The first thing is to press the finger of the left hand very hard into the fingerboard, stopping the string so firmly that it's almost like creating a new nut. This gives something closer to the resonance of an open string and avoids any impurity in the sound.

STEINHARDT   One should also take care that the right-hand action isn't too slow. Even when one is playing quietly in a slow tempo, the duration of the finger motion should be very quick; otherwise the string won't be adequately set in vibration. Vibrato is, of course, a crucial factor in ensuring both the continuation and beauty of sound.

DALLEY   It's important as well to pick the right spot on the string. Normally, if you want a full, resonant pizzicato you should choose a place in the upper part of the fingerboard, midway between the stopped note and the bridge, where the string is most supple.

When one is playing loudly it's best to pluck the string sideways rather than vertically; you'll get more resonance, and there is less chance of the string hitting the fingerboard. For a harder or drier sound, you can pluck the string more vertically and play nearer the bridge. So the quality of sound depends on a combination of many factors.

SOYER   The fact that pizzicato rings better on the cello than on the higher-voiced instruments poses another kind of problem. To match the sonority of the other players I often have to tone down my pizzicato, either by playing more softly or by choosing a less brilliant string.

For inexperienced players there's a danger of anticipating a pizzicato.

SOYER   Always—and for experienced players, too!

DALLEY   The main thing is to realize that the pizzicato produces an immediate response. In other words, the string is put into vibration more quickly than it would be by the bow, where there's a fraction of a second's delay. It's better to play almost behind the beat. Of course, the inner rhythm must be accurate.

TREE   Whenever possible—if I have enough time—I'll rest my thumb against the fingerboard and pluck with the first finger, meanwhile holding the bow in the palm of my hand. You can easily lose control if you don't use the fingerboard as a support. If you reach for the notes from midair, you risk hitting other strings. And coming from above doesn't make for as good a sound, because you can't get well in and under the string. Sometimes, though, special effects are called for, when you'll brush the string from above.

DALLEY   An example would be the harplike pizzicato chords in the Scherzo of the Ravel Quartet:

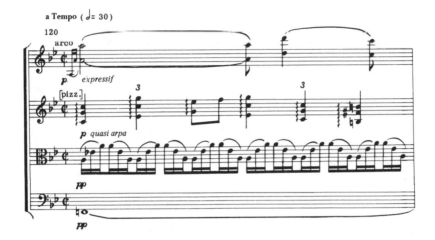

When playing this I roll my finger over the strings, using a circular motion in the manner of a jazz bass-player. I don't pluck the strings separately, but I have to be sure to catch each one and see to it that the upper notes stand out clearly. A lot of vibrato helps the resonance here.

TREE   Another piece of general advice: It's almost always helpful to play pizzicato one dynamic level above that which is indicated in the score. Pizzicato notes die away all too quickly; it's seldom that they are sufficiently heard, particularly in the lower registers.

Do you favor the use of open strings in pizzicato?

TREE   On occasion. But if you're not careful, they can sound a bit twangy. Mixing open-string notes into a passage that consists mainly of stopped notes will make for an unevenness in the length of vibration.

Bowing

One of the most fascinating aspects of a Guarneri Quartet performance is the variety of bow strokes you use, creating an enormous range of color and expression. May we now discuss the art of bowing in string-quartet playing?

STEINHARDT   I'd like first of all to clear up a misunderstanding that sometimes arises. You know, colleagues from another quartet once came backstage and asked, "Is it true that you're breaking up? It looks as if you and the second violin are fighting." I couldn't imagine what they were referring to. What had happened was that they had noticed John's bow going in the opposite direction from mine in a certain passage. If this had happened in their quartet it would have been out-and-out mutiny.

SOYER   That's a specialty of ours. In our quartet you'll often see everyone's bow doing something different. We don't worry about visual similarity so long as we achieve aural similarity when appropriate.

In your performance the other night of Schubert's "Death and the Maiden" Quartet, the theme of the slow movement took on an unearthly beauty. Such a mundane matter as Arnold and John bowing in opposite directions seemed inconsequential.

STEINHARDT   I guess we could sometimes organize such things better, but there are times when it is in fact more practical for us to go our own ways—when we need to arrive in different parts of the bow at the end of our respective passages.

Very often students—and, indeed, professionals—conceive of the basic categories of bowing—détaché, martelé, spiccato, etc.—in one-dimensional ways. Would you comment on this?

DALLEY   The bow is a many-faceted tool and should be used as such. It's helpful not to restrict yourself to conventional ways of doing things. Take, for instance, a spiccato stroke; it can be played in various ways with varying effect. It's useful to play spiccato right at the frog—even in a fast tempo—when you want the maximum attack on each note, as in the Finale of Haydn's Opus 76, No. 6, where a powerful repetitive hammering is called for:

Another kind of short spiccato stroke is needed for the accompanying eighths in piano at the beginning of Beethoven's Opus 18, No. 6:

These notes should have a bright, brittle quality. You want something sparkling, not a textbook spiccato. I play the figure in the upper middle of the bow—slightly higher up than where it would be most comfortable—in order to get a little more bite. The stroke has much more vertical than horizontal motion. The rosin flies.

STEINHARDT This stroke is particularly useful for an accompaniment figure that must be extremely articulate while a melody sings above it. The cracks between the notes allow the melodic line to shine through more clearly—as in the pianissimo passage in the Scherzo of Tchaikovsky's D-major Quartet [Opus 11], where the first violin and viola, marked "dolce," are accompanied by short notes in the second violin and cello:

TREE   That kind of crisp attack is reminiscent of Heifetz's spiccato, which was rather high-bouncing compared with most fiddlers'. In fact, if you sat near him when he played a spiccato passage, you heard so much extraneous sound that it seemed more scratch than notes. But it certainly didn't sound like that twenty feet away; one was aware only of a marvelous articulation.

DALLEY   At the other extreme from the short stroke we've been speaking of there's a long and singing spiccato. In the Allegro theme of the first movement of Mozart's "Dissonance" Quartet [K. 465] the accompanying eighths should be every bit as melodic as the first violin:

The stroke is horizontal, with the bow kept low to the string, the fingers and wrist of the right hand being rather elastic so as not to get too much dryness and grit. It's a kind of half-spiccato, half-détaché, which some people call a French détaché. Here I would play rather near the frog. The length of the stroke and the intensity of the vibrato follow the contours of the melody.

At the beginning of Beethoven's Opus 59, No. 1 the eighths are also singing yet of a somewhat different character:

This would be an example of an intermediate kind of spiccato—neither too short nor too long. By maintaining a rather neutral quality we give the cellist greater freedom to shape the phrase as he wishes. We even tone down our crescendos somewhat to ensure that the cello will always be heard as the leading voice.

TREE   Another stroke which we often use is an all-up-bow spiccato. It works ideally for short notes in piano in a lively tempo, such as the eighths in the Scherzo from Mendelssohn's E-minor Quartet [Opus 44, No. 2]:

DALLEY   This bowing is also useful in the Finale of the Mendelssohn Violin Concerto. It has an advantage over down/up in that the sound is exactly the same on every stroke. It's produced in the middle of the bow and is controlled mainly by the arm and hand joining together to make a small lateral circle. Once the stroke is set in motion, it can go on by itself indefinitely; the player need only sit back and enjoy it.

TREE   In the eighth notes that accompany the "Thème russe" in the Scherzo of Beethoven's Opus 59, No. 2 an all-up-bow spiccato provides just the right springing texture:

SOYER   When, at bar 104, the theme comes as a declamatory statement in fortissimo, we do something rather unorthodox and play all down-bows—not only because it gives added strength but because it forces us to hold the tempo back, to work harder at what we're doing:

DALLEY   In a passage such as the opening of Brahms's B-flat Quartet [Opus 67] one wants each note to be very short and, though piano, incisive and vibrant:

An ideal stroke to use here is the collé. This was characterized by Galamian as a pizzicato done with the bow. Rather than brushing the string as in a normal spiccato, the bow—thrown by the fingers—momentarily grips the string and then springs up. With the release of pressure the sound comes of itself.

In the forte response we lengthen the bow stroke a little so that the sound doesn't become too harsh; it should still retain something of a scherzando quality and not be overdramatic.

SOYER   The question often arises as to whether to play a passage on or off the string. The choice can vary so often, depending upon how one conceives the character of the music, that it's hardly possible to give examples here. One hint, though, which we can offer is that a change in length of bow stroke can sometimes give the impression of an alteration in dynamic intensity. An example would be the final Allegro section of Beethoven's Opus 74. Even though this begins forte and has sforzandos, we play it somewhat off the string. Then, at the *ff* [bar 191] we immediately play fully on the string. The sudden added length gives the *ff* the powerful sense of emphasis it needs.

In the *Grosse Fuge,* where one plays fortissimo for bars on end, a similar change in bowing length is indispensable in helping to create an ultimate sense of climax.

The opening motif of Beethoven's Opus 18, No. 1 presents a problem in bowing. Do you begin down- or up-bow?

SOYER   We've discussed that a great deal. We used to begin down-bow and try to articulate the two eighth notes as best we could, either by playing them with short marcato strokes or by coming back in two up-bows. But now we begin up-bow, which has the advantage of placing the two eighths in the lower part of the bow, where they can easily be played off the string.

STEINHARDT   Even when, later in the movement, the figure appears in forte, we still begin it up-bow. However, when, at bar 151, the figure comes in a series—

—it's obviously impossible to begin each bar up-bow. One can then either play both eighths up-bow, taking care to remain in the lower part of the bow, or alternate the strokes as they come and try to give the eighths equal articulation, whether at the point or at the frog.

Could we turn our attention now to sustained bow strokes? I previously referred to the "unearthly beauty" of your sonority when playing the theme of the slow movement of Schubert's "Death and the Maiden" Quartet. Leaving aside any possible metaphysical speculations, how do you obtain this?

DALLEY   One tries to find a color, as it were, halfway between heaven and earth. The bow moves across the string so lightly that the string doesn't speak completely; this produces a kind of floating, silvery sound, midway between the note itself and the harmonic. I would suggest play-

ing in the upper half of the bow, near the fingerboard, with a very flowing motion. The main thing, as you say, is the mysterious, unearthly
quality, and if a note doesn't speak too well, it doesn't greatly matter.

Would this kind of stroke be used fairly often in French music?

DALLEY Yes. For instance, at the beginning of the Ravel Quartet.
There's a lovely passage in the first movement of the Debussy Quartet
where we use a variant of this bowing:

In these running sixteenth notes, beginning *pp* and then rising and falling, I imagine a sound like wind whistling through the trees. We play
very softly, not making too much of the crescendos and diminuendos,
so that the first-violin melody is able to stand out in relief. The left hand
must be extremely accurate. Our bows move lightly and rapidly—except that rather than playing over the fingerboard, as would be normal
in flautando, we play near the bridge. This creates a quasi-ponticello—
not a true ponticello, as there is none marked in the score, but only a
little of that color, enough to give an unusual clarity. I recently coached
an excellent quartet in this work. They played the passage well, but they
didn't achieve any of this mystery. When they thought of it in these
terms and tried this bowing, the passage was elevated from something
mundane and was invested with a kind of supernatural quality.

*Nonprofessionals seeing "piano" will often automatically react by playing with
very little bow.*

SOYER That's a mistake. Just as an actor has to make sure that his whis-

per is heard at the very back of the theatre, we must imagine our piano
being heard over a great distance. The quality of tone must project, and
using more bow—that is, moving the bow at a faster speed—is a great
help in this respect. When you want a transparent tone—as in the
"Death and the Maiden" theme—if the bow flows rather swiftly across
the string, it ensures that the sound will be more alive.

DALLEY   There are, of course, situations where the bow must move
slowly in piano. One of these is the Adagio of Schubert's C-major
Quintet, where each bow stroke has to last for the duration of a very
long bar. We resist the temptation to change the bow in the middle of
the bar, although it would make things a lot more comfortable. The
sustained bowing is attainable, though somewhat nerve-racking to execute. It isn't advisable to play over the fingerboard here; the bow is moving too slowly. One must play rather near to the bridge, where the
sound is more concentrated—more intense. And this, in fact, creates
just the proper sonority for the piece; it conveys a kind of inner anguish.
Maybe Schubert realized all this. When composers write in the white
heat of inspiration, they don't always foresee the problems of performance. But here the end and the means are ideally matched.

STEINHARDT   Sometimes you have to choose in favor of a difficult bowing. George Szell often imposed terribly difficult bowings on the Cleveland Orchestra. These were designed to ensure that the musical idea
would come through and to avert potential problems. One often has to
go far out of one's way, for instance, to obtain clear articulation. Now,
Carl Flesch in his excellent treatise *The Art of Violin Playing* advises al-
tering Beethoven's original slurring in Opus 18, No. 6 from

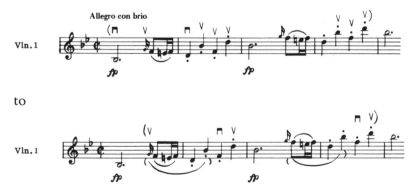

to

and applies this principle to similar passages. It's tempting to make the
change; it's musical, and comfortable from an instrumental point of

view. Yet I prefer the original; it ensures that the figure will be clearly etched, which can be of considerable importance when playing in a large hall. I'd rather sacrifice ease for character. The rapid change of bow here makes you work harder; you're cursing all along, but you're articulating.

SOYER One of the most persistent challenges to bowing—as it is to left-hand technique—is the articulation of quick notes that follow a long note, particularly when they're within the same legato slur.

STEINHARDT As a rule, string players are taught to play as smoothly as possible, to treat the bow as if it were dipped in oil. At times that can be self-defeating. In the following passage—darkly textured and marked crescendo—from the Minuet of Beethoven's Opus 18, No. 5, if one doesn't make a "wrong" accent, the first note of the turn in bar 41 is simply not heard, for acoustical reasons:

When first tried, such accents may seem unmusical, but experience will show that quick notes which you might have thought to be clear when practicing tend to be swallowed up in a concert hall; you have to take great pains—unmusical pains!—to make sure that they're heard.

TREE Another example of an intentional "wrong" accent is found in the rhythmic figure, favored by Beethoven, which dominates the Finale of Opus 59, No. 2:

One must consciously articulate the eighth note. When this figure is played slowly, the accent might sound overstated, but when it is taken up to tempo, the eighth doesn't seem exaggeratedly strong but only as equally clear as the quarter. We usually play this figure near the point with a down/up motion, the down-bow coming on the eighth. This gives the right articulation and the natural rhythmic vitality.

DALLEY　The rhythmic élan is inherent in the bow stroke. The eighth note comes just a hair's breadth later and faster than marked. If you play that rhythm mathematically "correct" as it appears on paper, you'll lose a little of the energy in the stroke. I think that Beethoven understood how such figures would be played on stringed instruments; the sense of rhythmic vitality is part and parcel of his conception.

Hearing you play this movement, one is struck by the tremendous drive and concision in your performance. Technically, how do you execute the repetitive rhythmic figure, and is it tiring for the bow arm?

TREE　It's not primarily an arm motion; it's basically a finger motion. The down/up comes together in one reflex; the bow grips the string and is then released. Actually, it's not tiring. We could play this movement two or three times in a row.

STEINHARDT　Speak for yourself, Michael.

SOYER　It's somewhat tiring, played, as it is, at the point. For the cellist most of the impetus comes from the forearm, although there's some flexibility in the fingers. It helps to have the feeling that the down-bow strokes bite the string in a vertical rather than a horizontal sense.

DALLEY　I disagree with Michael. I don't think the fingers come much into play in this particular stroke. I play it with the arm.

STEINHARDT　When the figure comes in forte I, too, think that the bulk of the motion has really to come from the arm. But as the arm is relatively slow moving, there should be a looseness in the wrist and fingers to help with the snap. It's a bit like flicking a whip.

DALLEY　There are other passages, of course, where we don't want to emphasize the short notes, where there's a risk of their being too obtrusive.

TREE　Take the Trio of the Minuet of Beethoven's Opus 18, No. 5:

In order to avoid wrong accents here we use what we call a "hooked" bowing. For instance, in the third bar we take two down-bows. (These don't imply a legato; we make a slight articulation.) In this way we're not forced to take an unnecessarily long stroke for the first note. In the fourth bar, by taking two up-bows we avoid the necessity of using a whole bow for the first two notes; these should be understated prior to the sforzando. The final sforzando [bar 6] is joined in a legato slur to the subsequent bar. This is a rather unorthodox bowing, but we find that it's well suited to the musical intention.

STEINHARDT   Another example would be the third movement of Beethoven's Opus 59, No. 2:

The hooked bowing economizes motion and ensures that the detached eighth notes won't be accented or come late, as might tend to be the case if the bow had to be retaken.

I trust that you're all in agreement about this particular bowing.

DALLEY   About the bowing, yes—but not about the tempo! To get the whole truth you should interrogate us separately, as they do in police stations.

Note Lengths

When we discussed variety in bow strokes, we dealt with choices that have to be made in the lengths of notes. Let's take a further look at the question of note lengths—for instance, the interpretation of so-called staccato dots.

SOYER   There's a widespread misunderstanding that a dot over a note means that the note should necessarily be short. However, in the time of Mozart and Beethoven a dot meant simply a separation; it was just a way of indicating that a note wasn't to be sustained all the way through. The note can be short, medium short, or medium long, according to its context.

STEINHARDT   Sometimes it's not only a question of the amount of space between notes; a dot can imply a kind of lilt. Take the upbeat to Mozart's A-major String Quartet [K. 464]:

That note seems to want to breathe. It's a loving dot; the bow should caress the string in a swaying motion. If the note is played too short it's a mockery of Mozart's intention.

A series of notes of equal written value may tend to sound monotonous. They will often benefit from a variety in length of stroke in accordance with the melodic and harmonic intent. A typical example is found in the Minuet from Beethoven's Opus 18, No. 5:

DALLEY   Variety in note lengths is crucial to such a theme as the second subject of the first movement of Beethoven's Opus 18, No. 2:

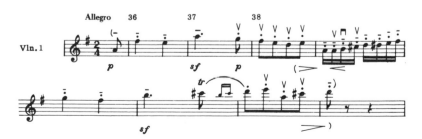

We play the eighth-note upbeat with a half-singing quality; there's a lot of air in the stroke. The two quarters in bar 36 are rather long, the bow being only slightly lifted. In bar 37 the dotted quarter is sustained to avoid breaking the line of the phrase. The eighth notes in bar 38 are on the short side, with a scherzando quality, and the sixteenths that follow are slightly longer again to bridge over to the next phrase. If one were careless one might play all the notes equally short, and this lovely theme would sound brittle and square.

STEINHARDT Sometimes a figure will undergo many transformations during the course of a movement, and you may want to vary the length of the notes accordingly. In the second movement of Beethoven's Opus 18, No. 4 we play the motif of repeated eighth notes by turn short and giocoso—

—slightly elongated and quasi espressivo—

—sustained and dramatic—

—portato—

—portato in the first violin while simultaneously short and giocoso in the second violin—

—a little longer than at the beginning—with a gracious lilt, as if saying farewell—

TREE   However, these indications shouldn't be inscribed on tablets for the ages. With the Guarneri Quartet the dots can change between San Francisco and Los Angeles.

SOYER   The dots in Los Angeles are vastly different from those anywhere else!

Beethoven is sometimes explicit as to where there is a dot and where there is not. In the second subject to the first movement of Opus 18, No. 5—

—the upbeat to bar 25 has a dot, but not that to bar 27; by sustaining this second upbeat one brings greater continuity and warmth to the theme.

In the five-note motif that wends its way through the Allegro of the first movement of Beethoven's Opus 130, one usually hears the two eighth notes played spiccato, though there are no dots over them in the score. You play these eighths on the string, and this seemingly small difference has a considerable influence on the character of the movement; the motif takes on greater strength in forte and more serenity in piano:

SOYER   My colleagues feel as you do, although I myself would have preferred to have the eighths shorter.

STEINHARDT   Although we do play the eighths at the point, we take care to give them a little articulation. This figure is disarmingly simple, isn't it? Not a tune, really, but a little signal, like Morse code.

DALLEY   In the slow movement of Opus 59, No. 2 Beethoven goes out of his way to indicate three ways in which the length of the dotted-note motif should be interpreted: as a melody, fully sustained—

—as an accompaniment of mainly rhythmic character (as in the slow movement of the Fourth Symphony), the bow being stopped and the sixteenth well articulated—

—and as part melody, part accompaniment, the note length being somewhere between the two previous examples—

STEINHARDT In this last-mentioned figure, the separation between notes should be only very slight. I also like to allow for a degree of variability; as the phrase evolves, some notes need a little more length than others. The most important determining factor in interpretation should always be the musical context rather than simply the way in which the notes are written. But Beethoven's notation in this movement does, of course, provide very helpful guidelines.

Another special notation in Beethoven, but this time far more enigmatic, is the slur he places over notes of identical pitch and of equal time value, as found, for instance, in the Grosse Fuge—

—and used as well in the Quartets, Opus 74, 130, 131, and 132. How do you interpret this marking?

TREE Now we're getting into something very delicate. We all agree that something should be done, but not on what should be done. Interpreters of Beethoven have struggled with this question for more than a century and a half.

DALLEY Beethoven seems to want something between one note and two notes, possibly a double pulsation. I would prefer to make these pulsations with the vibrato, because it's hard to keep from doing too much if you make two impulses with the bow.

STEINHARDT I've experimented with different possibilities. One idea is to make a kind of swell from the first note to the second—the sort one hears from players who've fallen into the bad musical habit of unconsciously making a crescendo after the beginning of a bow stroke. Another idea—the one I have adopted here—is to make the second note an echo of the first, like an immediate rebound of a softer quality. The essential thing is to convey a sense of tremulous agitation.

In the Piano Sonata, Opus 110, Beethoven has a similar notation; he indicates a change of fingering—4–3—for the two slurred notes:*

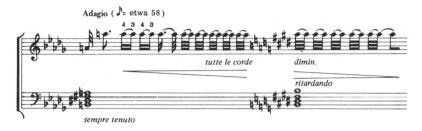

I asked Menahem Pressler about this passage. He says that although an echolike rebound was easier to achieve on the piano of Beethoven's day, with its lighter-weight hammers, the effect can be achieved on the modern piano "if you practice with care and have rubber fingers." In a footnote to this passage in his edition of Beethoven's piano sonatas Artur Schnabel wrote: "The key which is touched by the third finger, should produce a tone hovering between reality and imagination—but must be heard, none the less. Perhaps it might be helpful to take some suitable word for this pair, a monosyllable, such as Du, whose vowel takes on a soulful emphasis."

STEINHARDT These comments are very interesting indeed; Schnabel's words admirably express what the first violin should try to achieve when stating the *Grosse Fuge* subject in pianissimo. A question then arises as to what to do with the same figure when it appears repeatedly in fortissimo.

TREE The danger is that after the impact of the first of the slurred notes, you'll want the second note to be equally well heard through the thick texture; you'll thus make too great an effort and end up playing two distinct, equal notes. We don't think that was Beethoven's intent. So when the figure occurs in fortissimo, we feel that it's better to let it simply sound as a quarter note.

STEINHARDT That's at least our official policy for the present, but I'm not quite convinced that some sort of shading shouldn't be done. And later, when the figure enters on a syncopation, one could make a crescendo leading to the main beat—which I mentioned as one of the possibilities.

* A 4–3 fingering is also indicated over tied notes in the slow movement of the "Hammerklavier" Sonata, Opus 106, and in the piano part of the Scherzo of the Cello Sonata, Opus 69; in these cases the figure begins on a syncopation.

SOYER   There's no certainty that Beethoven meant the figure to be interpreted in the same way in every case.

TREE   The last chord of the Cavatina from Opus 130 is divided into four eighths joined by slurs, and here we do give each eighth a little emphasis with the bow:

There's a passage relevant to this in Mendelssohn's A-major Quartet, Opus 13, written in the year of Beethoven's death.

SOYER   That piece is one of my favorites. Many of its ideas are consciously patterned on passages from the late Beethoven quartets; it's a kind of homage.

The closing bars are, as you know, a recollection of the ending of the Cavatina; Mendelssohn even uses similar slurs from note to note. But—significantly—he adds accents which don't appear in the Beethoven:

These accents may be Mendelssohn's interpretation of Beethoven's intention; in other words, they show that he felt there should be an expressive pulsation on each note. Although Mendelssohn may not have heard Beethoven's Opus 130 performed, he may have been acquainted with a tradition in the performance of such slurs in Beethoven's works, or he may simply have read Beethoven's score with his musical intuition.

SOYER That's a very good piece of detective work on your part. Mendelssohn was certainly closer to the scene than we are; I think his accents are undoubtedly right in reference to the ending of the Cavatina. The question is whether they would also be valid for the *Grosse Fuge.* It's a quandary.

I have an amusing story about this. Some years ago I met a girl who claimed to be a clairvoyant and to have spoken with Dante. I asked her if she thought she could also speak with Beethoven, and she said, "I don't see why not. What is it you would like to know?" I wrote out one of these examples of slurs over two notes and put a big question mark next to it. Several weeks later I ran into her. "I've just spoken with Beethoven," she said. "I'm never going to do that again. He was very unpleasant; he's short, has a rough voice—and I don't even speak German. But I showed him what you had written and he sang the answer. It sounded like this: '*uhh-uhh . . . uhh-uhh.*'" This girl had had no musical training and couldn't possibly have known what the notation meant.

So there you have it . . .

SOYER Right from the horse's mouth. It's as good an answer as we've been able to come up with after twenty years.

TREE While speaking of note lengths, I'd like to put a word in for *rest* lengths. Players too often allow silences to occur haphazardly. There's an unconscious tendency to lunge forward and let the music enter with a syncopated effect. When that happens it's a sure sign that one hasn't subdivided the rhythm inwardly. Rests have a dramatic impact of their own. During the long silences in the slow movement of Beethoven's Opus 18, No. 1 [see page 13] every eighth-note beat has to be fully accounted for.

SOYER I remember a rehearsal of the NBC Symphony when Toscanini stopped Heifetz during the cadenza of the Beethoven Violin Concerto because Heifetz had anticipated by a hair's breadth the entrance of the repeated sixteenths after the rests:

Strictly speaking, the cadenza was not Toscanini's concern; but he held up a warning finger and said, "Count the rests; play when the bar line comes—not before."

Textual Clarifications

Toscanini was renowned for his adherence to the printed score. Even he, however, occasionally made small textual alterations when he felt they were necessary for the sake of clearer orchestral texture. Do you find that such changes are sometimes needed in the quartet literature?

STEINHARDT   It's very, very rare that we make any sort of change. But the exceptions prove the rule. There are two passages in Beethoven's quartets where, without changing the actual notes, we alter the distribution of voices for better thematic clarity. The first is near the end of the Finale of Opus 18, No. 5:

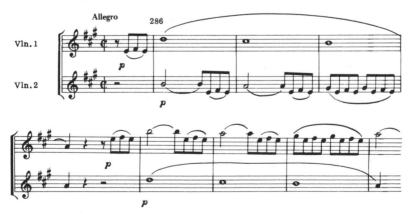

The second and the first violin in turn play identical four-bar phrases (the first violin being an octave higher). In the score, however, the first violin is given the three-note upbeat figure both times. If this is indeed

Beethoven speaking, and not a mistake in the first edition, I don't understand the logic. We've decided that the second violin should play the first upbeat figure, which is, after all, an intrinsic part of its melody. We thus rearrange the score as follows:

DALLEY   We also make a small change in Opus 127. Just before the end of the main section of the Scherzo, Beethoven breaks up the melody by dividing it between the viola and the second violin. Since the second violin plays double-stops in bars 139–140, the main voice tends to be obscured:

We allow the viola to take the whole line. In other words, the second violin and the viola exchange their A flat and F:

STEINHARDT   Although this is perfectly logical and sounds better, I do have a guilty conscience about the change. The improvement is so obvious that I wonder why Beethoven composed it as he did. He may have had a reason for it.

TREE   It may have been just a simple miscalculation.

The miracle is that there are so few miscalculations in his quartets.

TREE   In practical terms, we believe it serves his purpose better to make that adjustment; as it's only on one sixteenth note, we're hardly being cavalier with the text. However, every case has to be considered on its merits and tried out in performance. There are various passages where we thought a change might be worthwhile but finally decided against it.

STEINHARDT   We do occasionally alter the distribution of chords. Three-note chords sometimes present problems. If one really concentrates on playing all the notes faithfully, the top note may suffer—the very note that's generally of greatest melodic importance.

Bruno Walter dealt with chords in an orchestra by requesting that they be played divisi, with the outside player taking only the top note and the inside player the two bottom notes.

STEINHARDT   An excellent idea.

Obviously the quartet can't play divisi—

STEINHARDT   No, but we can nonetheless make certain adjustments, especially in avoiding unnecessary doublings. The opening of Beethoven's Opus 59, No. 2 provides an example:

The bottom E in the first violin is duplicated in the viola part. This allows me the luxury of favoring the upper two notes to advantage. I may not even officially notify myself that I'm leaving out the lowest note; if it speaks, fine; if it doesn't, it's not too serious a loss.

DALLEY   I leave out the high E in my first chord to avoid duplicating the first violin; there shouldn't be a preponderance of open-string E's.

STEINHARDT   The opening of the Scherzo of Beethoven's Opus 127 poses a similar problem:

In a three-note pizzicato chord, the last-played note tends to be the least heard. If I attempt to play all three notes in each of these pizzicato chords, the melodically important upper note will be much too weak. Fortunately, all my middle and lower notes are doubled by other instruments, excepting the first low G, which can be taken by the second violin. This allows me to play only the two upper notes. True, you lose something in the way of fullness, but you gain a great deal in melodic clarity.

TREE   Aside from the question of doubling notes, a composer will sometimes write chords which are awkward to play. In a chord containing the interval of a fifth there's a risk of poor intonation because of the necessity to lay one finger across two strings. In such cases it's sometimes helpful to rewrite the chord, preserving the same notes but redistributing them among the players so that the fingering is less problematic. Difficulties arise, too, with four-note chords which shouldn't sound broken. We'll sometimes redistribute the chord or thin it out slightly by reducing the doubling.

STEINHARDT   When contemplating making such an alteration, one must always be careful, because the composer may have had a specific sonority in mind. We've sometimes rewritten a chord and have been pleased with the improvement in intonation but have found that the timbre suffers; it may lack the focus or the resonance of the original. We've then decided to retain the original version, even though it may be far more difficult to execute.

TREE   We sometimes take a slight liberty which I wouldn't even characterize as an alteration. One often has a powerful forte note to attack from the air. If the note happens to be on a middle string, one feels slightly inhibited for fear that the bow might inadvertently touch on other strings. If the note in question happens to have its counterpart on an adjacent open string, we'll let the bow come down on both strings simultaneously, and then—to avoid the double-stop being heard—immediately leave the open string. Nobody is aware of it; it just allows the attack to be more abandoned. We find such instances in the Scherzo of Beethoven's Opus 74 [see bars 86 and 97]—

—and in the opening viola solo in Smetana's *From My Life* [bar 7]:

Dynamics

One still encounters a basic misunderstanding about "textual fidelity" when it comes to dynamics. There's a world of difference between reading a score literally and understanding it creatively. For instance, in your performances you interpret the indication "piano" with a great deal of latitude.

SOYER   Yes. Nuances are not meant to be something static; they must be perceived in their context. As Casals used to say, "'Piano' is a *range* of sound; it can have a wide variation."

TREE   In other words, "piano" is a very relative marking.

DALLEY   Especially for the viola.

TREE   I hope our readers will catch on to our warped sense of humor.

SOYER   I'm not sure they'll want to. In any case, markings are black on white, but music wasn't meant to sound that way. It's often the case that a crescendo or a diminuendo has to be adjusted to the demands of the overall line. In the slow movement of Beethoven's Opus 59, No. 2 I have a repeated figure—an expressive octave leap—that begins piano and yet is supposed to subside to pianissimo four bars later:

If I were to take the piano marking literally, the diminuendo would have nowhere to go, and the passage would become static. To avoid letting the tension down completely, I begin with more tone. Even when the passage is played above the marking, it won't sound loud compared with the previous forte. Besides, everybody drops out and the cello is left alone. I then allow each of the succeeding figures to diminish gradually until arriving at *ppp*.

It's clear from your performances that when Beethoven writes pp *you infer a special meaning—a certain intimacy or mystery.*

TREE   Yes. Beethoven's pianissimo usually implies more than just a change in dynamics; it has to do with harmonic shading, with atmosphere. We make a point of contrasting pianissimo with piano, and if the pianissimo seems especially soft, it may in large measure be due to the fact that the previous piano hasn't been understated. Of course, not every composer uses "pianissimo" with the specific intent that Beethoven does. Verdi, for instance, marks *ppp* time and again in his quartet. This was, as we know, his way of compensating for the tendency of the musicians with whom he worked to play too loudly.

Toscanini always insisted that the Verdi pianissimo should not be exaggerated, and requested a normal singing tone.

DALLEY The proof of this is in the music itself. Verdi often has such markings in passages which are extremely difficult and uncomfortable to play in a true pianissimo. Beethoven, on the other hand, writes *pp* in passages that are intrinsically suited to pianissimo interpretation.

STEINHARDT Let's not forget that Beethoven makes a clear distinction at the other end of the dynamic range, between *f* and *ff*. We'll often go out of our way in a forte passage to heighten this contrast by making a slight diminuendo just before a fortissimo, so that it's thrown more sharply into relief.

DALLEY In the first movement of Opus 95, the diminuendos give definition to the sforzandos and allow the *ff* to enter with new vigor.

If, on the other hand, we have a forte or a crescendo followed by a subito piano, we might rise to the very end, giving the impression that we're about to reach our peak, and only at the last moment go over to piano. Of course, there are many lyrical passages where one wants to take care that the subito piano doesn't break the melodic continuity. An example would be found in the Cavatina from Opus 130 [see page 48]. In this case we don't stop the bow before the piano but glide from one nuance to the other, often taking a shade of extra time in doing so.

SOYER Beethoven sometimes indicates *pp* followed by a crescendo and a *p*. The question then arises as to whether a subito *p* is actually intended. I remember Toscanini arriving at a rehearsal one day, hitting himself on the head and crying out, "*Stupido!*" He told us that he had been studying the crescendo in the choralelike passage near the end of the *Pastoral* Symphony and suddenly realized that a subito piano is not implied. "It's no more than a crescendo from pianissimo to piano," he exclaimed, "not a crescendo *beyond* piano! How could I have failed to see it all these years?"

We treat the following passages similarly—that is, our crescendo doesn't go beyond piano. We interpret the *p* to be on the upper scale of its range, and not a sudden decrease of dynamic intensity:

Beethoven, Opus 18, No. 3, second movement

Beethoven, Opus 127, second movement

Such decisions are, however, not cut and dried; they are often a matter of intuition. Sometimes we don't agree on the meaning of a marking. There's one such place in the slow movement of Beethoven's Opus 59, No. 2:

I personally don't believe that a subito *ff* is implied in bar 58 but, rather, that the crescendo is meant to carry through to the *ff*. I'm outvoted, however, and we do make a subito *ff*.

DALLEY   For my part, I find it characteristic of Beethoven—who loved the unexpected—to make a crescendo to *f* and then surprise us with a subito *ff*.

A marking which is frequently misunderstood is the sforzando. One shouldn't forget that a sforzando's intensity is always relative to its dynamic and expressive context. For instance, the four sforzandos in the first movement of Beethoven's Opus 18, No. 1 are often overplayed. The dynamic marking "piano" carries over from the previous passage. The *ff* in bar 100 is meant to come as a surprise.

These sforzandos retain, in any case, a certain nervous energy in keeping with the agitated mood. However, some sforzandos should be treated so as not to disrupt the lyrical line. They're more an expressive left-hand articulation than an accent with the bow:

Beethoven, Opus 18, No. 3, first movement

TREE   In the second movement of Beethoven's Opus 59, No. 3 we find *sfp* in pianissimo:

The atmosphere is hushed to the point of being sinister; the *sfp* should be no more than a muted shudder; the bow just touches the string.

SOYER   Beethoven often indicates a series of sforzandos, particularly in vigorous passages. These reiterations can sometimes be thought of as having a cumulative effect and implying a crescendo. We don't make a rule about it. But whatever one does, it's important to avoid monotony.

DALLEY   Dynamics again require special attention when a phrase is divided up into segments taken in turn by different instruments. In a passage such as the following, from the first movement of Beethoven's Opus 59, No. 2—

—the segments should sound connected, as if they are being played by a single instrument. Thus the dynamic level should be as even as possible. Each player must resist the temptation to let his segment taper off in diminuendo and should sustain his last note until the moment when the next voice enters. The entering player should take care not to overemphasize his first note.

STEINHARDT   The gradation of dynamics is particularly delicate when the segments join in an overall crescendo or diminuendo:

Beethoven, Opus 59, No. 1, first movement

A player's natural inclination when seeing a crescendo is to begin softly and end loudly, but it's important to know just where your segment lies in the overall scheme. Perhaps you're the second link in the chain, in which case it may be your role to carry the line from *mp* to *mf*.

TREE   The trick in segmented passages is to play all the parts mentally while actually playing only one of them. The player who is about to enter should already be in motion, breathing, as it were, with the previous voice. At such times it's not enough simply to enter in tempo. You're joining a stream of traffic just as if you had been waiting at a stop sign and suddenly have to pull out onto a major thoroughfare and keep up with the cars whizzing by. You'll have to anticipate your entrance a little, or you're almost bound to come in late.

DALLEY   Sometimes one has a series of segments all to oneself, as in the accompaniment figure in the Minuet from Beethoven's Opus 18, No. 5:

The risk is that each bar will sound like an entity in itself. So I try to give the passage a sense of melodic continuity by bringing together groups of two or four bars, depending on the phrasing of the first violin. Using long, floating bows, I fully sustain the A at the end of the first bar and let the sound carry through so that the quarter-note rest at the beginning of the second bar doesn't seem to break the line. From bar 5 Arnold may build the line in terraces as the phrase mounts; I'll respond accordingly.

SOYER   One must also look for continuity in the theme of the Scherzo
from Beethoven's Opus 127:

Each statement of the four-note motif retains its identity yet should be
perceived as part of the overall line shared by the cello and viola. Within
the motif itself I feel in the upbeats a slight leaning, both dynamic and
rhythmic, towards the quarter note, which, in turn, has a diminuendo.
However, the segments don't remain static; they rise in terraces with a
slight increase in dynamic intensity.

TREE   I phrase each bar just as Dave does, but since mine is the descending line, I allow a gradual diminuendo. Thus, although the only dynamic marking is *pp,* an arc is drawn in a subtle way over the entire
eight-bar period.

How poverty-stricken we are with our half-dozen dynamic indications!

STEINHARDT   Yes—but, paradoxically, the very primitivity of the system may have a value in that it forces us to search for the answers ourselves.

TREE   In a way, things become more problematic when composers
overmark their music, appending instructions to virtually every note, as
Berg and Webern did. The performer isn't trusted to do anything on his
own. It drives you to distraction trying to be so literal; it binds you
down.

Even when the score is marked in so complex a way, it's still not possible to represent the real moment-to-moment life of nuances which are too subtle for any kind of existing notation.

STEINHARDT   Josef Hofmann was once approached by a piano-roll manufacturer with a request to make a recording. He declined, saying that such a machine couldn't possibly do justice to his range of dynamics. "But," replied the manufacturer, "I want you to know that our piano rolls have seventeen degrees of dynamics." Hofmann said, "Thank you very much; I'm sorry, but I happen to have eighteen."

Rhythm; Tempo

TREE   If the printed score fails to convey the subtleties of dynamics, rhythmic values don't fare much better. It's often the case that notation tells us little of the real essence of a rhythm. This is particularly true of the relationship between short and long notes.

SOYER   Take the beginning of Beethoven's Opus 18, No. 2, which contrasts the melodic graciousness of the opening figure with the rhythmic vitality of the motif that follows:*

The thirty-second-note upbeats gain in vitality if they're slightly delayed and played a little more quickly than written. Casals used to call this a "natural rhythm," as opposed to a printed rhythm. We think of each

---

* The arrows in this and the following musical examples suggest this sense of forward rhythmic direction.

thirty-second note here as being attached to its coming neighbor, the skeletal structure consisting of the eighth notes falling on the main beats, with the short notes being in the nature of embellishments.

DALLEY   One could cite innumerable cases where the rhythmic intensity is heightened by a very subtle concision of the short note in relation to the long. We've already mentioned the Finale of Beethoven's Opus 59, No. 2 in this respect. The following are other examples:

Mozart, Quartet in D minor, K. 421, Finale

Schubert, Quartet in D minor, Finale

Schumann, Quartet in A major, Opus 41, No. 3, Finale

SOYER   Sometimes two shorter notes will have a sense of momentum leading to a longer note. The cello figure towards the end of the Andante of Mozart's A-major Quartet [K. 464] has a piquant quality:

It gains in vitality if the two thirty-second notes come slightly late and fast. Similarly, in the cello solo that begins the second movement of Beethoven's Opus 59, No. 1, I try to convey a sense of lilt, not merely a series of repeated notes:

Vlc.

The two sixteenths can be slightly compressed—in other words, played a shade quicker than notated, there being the tiniest wait between the two eighth notes. There's a slight tapering off in each of the first two bars. I envisage the points of rhythmic emphasis over the four bars as: *one–one–one, two, three–one.* This pattern is often found in rustic Ländler and is also characteristic of many minuets by Haydn and Mozart.

TREE The length of short notes is always subject to the nature of the piece. When the character is expressive and lyrical, we might go out of our way to emphasize their sustained quality. In the slow movement of Beethoven's Opus 132 we'll take enough time to sing on the sixteenth notes, even if it means stretching the rhythm slightly:

Vln. 2

SOYER Arthur Rubinstein frequently elongated short notes in this way. It was one of the secrets of his wonderful lyricism.

DALLEY It's clear that short notes often require a degree of flexibility in one direction or another. The important thing is to get to the essence of the music and not be bound literally to the printed notation.

It's a particular characteristic of the Guarneri Quartet to allow a degree of flexibility, where appropriate, within the overall tempo.

STEINHARDT Maybe, as I've said, we're a little old-fashioned. We do tend to allow more freedom in this respect than most string quartets today. Ideally, one wants to find a tempo that reconciles all the diverse elements within a movement. But sometimes this proves impossible, and a certain amount of tempo modification is desirable. We're not dogmatic about tempo regularity. In variation movements, for example, we'll often allow the tempo a wide latitude. Most music requires some flexibility up to a point, unless we're playing something like the Stravinsky Concertino—the machine age with steel rods moving up and down—where there's no room for such pleasantries.

SOYER   Every movement has an overall pulse, but we feel that within the basic tempo there's room for a certain elasticity. It's somewhat like the question of dynamics. Just as "piano" has a broad range, the basic tempo can have a range of movement. While we try not to go to extremes, we're not afraid of that flexibility.

DALLEY   An example of this sort of elasticity of pulse would be the beginning of the "Heiliger Dankgesang" from Beethoven's Opus 132 [see page 38]. We feel that the quarter-note passages have an inherent linear quality and sense of ongoing motion; the chorale itself should be more sustained, the motion being held back almost as if suspended in time.

STEINHARDT   Some musicians, however, are very strict about this sort of thing. As a young man I studied the Beethoven Violin Concerto with George Szell. When I wanted to take more time during the lyrical G-minor section in the development of the first movement, he became furious with me, finding it maudlin and disruptive of the architectural structure; he insisted that I play it absolutely in tempo at the concert. Szell could on occasion let himself go and change tempos, but he probably thought I was terribly self-indulgent and needed to be taught a lesson. In that sense his influence was salutary—though I still haven't lost a certain liking for some of the same excesses.

SOYER   By way of contrast, I recall an occasion when we were rehearsing in Paris with Arthur Rubinstein. He was practicing the Scherzo of the Fauré Piano Quartet in G minor. I drew his attention to the fact that he was playing it much more slowly than the metronome marking. He turned the metronome on, checked the tempo, and said, "Oh, yes, but that's only for the first bar." The story is amusing, but it's also to be taken seriously.

DALLEY   Obviously, every movement has its own character; some are more susceptible than others to fluctuations of tempo. Sometimes, particularly in scherzos and finales, a consistent rhythmic impulse is a predominant feature. In certain cases the modifications are so subtle as to be barely thought of as modifications at all. Take the first movement of Beethoven's Opus 18, No. 1. We allow a certain suppleness in the lyrical moments and when modulating into remote keys, but we have to be careful not to take too much time. The movement as a whole has a sort of nervous energy; one shouldn't get too far away from the propelling rhythmic force.

TREE When we do feel that a certain passage—a second subject, for instance—requires considerably more time than the main tempo allows, we're very much aware of the need to maintain a sense of structural integrity despite the tempo change. One has to determine at exactly what points the tempo can be relaxed, and eventually retaken, in the most natural way.

Bruno Walter used to speak of "apparent continuity of tempo."

STEINHARDT A wonderful expression! That's just what one should always strive for.

May we have an example?

SOYER How about the second subject of the first movement of Beethoven's Opus 130? It may be due to the self-indulgence that Arnold mentioned, but we like a more relaxed tempo there.

TREE Putting the shoe on the other foot, is there any reason to play all that material in the main tempo? The character changes drastically.

DALLEY   In this case Beethoven seems to invite a slackening of pace in the passage of eighth notes [bars 51–52] leading into the cello solo.

SOYER   My sixteenth notes [bars 53–54] are legato, in D-flat major, sotto voce. It's a moment of quiet reflection and shouldn't be hurried.

STEINHARDT   In bars 55–57 I take enough time for my phrase to sing expressively, after which the cello regains a slightly more flowing motion [bars 57–58], making a bridge to the next violin statement. Then, at bar 63, Beethoven provides a natural opportunity to retake the main tempo.

TREE   The question of tempo is a delicate one throughout this movement, owing to the frequent alternation of Adagio ma non troppo and Allegro. It's important that the opening Adagio and its recurrences not be too slow; the "ma non troppo" must be kept in mind. To dwell endlessly on those passages pulls apart the fabric of the piece. It borders on the maudlin if you try to squeeze every ounce of meaning out of it.

STEINHARDT   Two movements come to mind that are particularly interesting from the standpoint of tempo. Owing to its fantasylike, rhapsodic character, the first movement of Beethoven's Opus 59, No. 2 has generated more discussion among us about tempo than any other movement in the "Razumovsky" quartets. Immediately there's a sense of give and take. The chords set the tempo defiantly:

If anything, we elongate the rests to emphasize the effect of the halting motion. Beethoven often uses rests to increase the sense of expectancy. Here they seem to be asking, "What's going to happen next?" In between the rests each *pp* passage is drawn together in a tight rhythmic grouping, like excited whispering.

SOYER   This movement hardly ever lets up. It's like a stream constantly running over rocks and rushing down in little torrents and cascades. The tempo has to be very flexible, but the extent of modification isn't extreme. Even in the lyrical second subject there's still this sense of ongoing motion.

STEINHARDT   At the beginning of the development (and of the coda) the modulations are arresting; one needs a moment to mull them over in one's mind. We take a little more time, particularly at the enharmonic change [bar 74]:

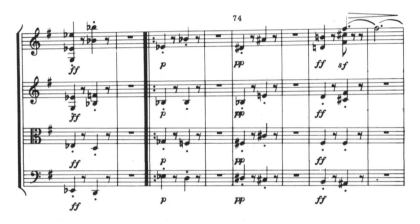

But the torrents continue. We end the movement strictly in tempo: concise, breathless, and without sentimentality.

STEINHARDT   The first movement of Opus 95 is even more wild and turbulent.

DALLEY   This is one of my favorite quartets. The first movement is unique in its extraordinary terseness, its harmonic boldness, and its rapid changes of mood—fierce one moment, tender the next. No other movement having only a single tempo mark calls out for so many fluctuations of speed within such short time spans.

TREE   We feel the opening two bars in one sweep and play the eighths all up-bow—almost like an immediate accelerando. In the answering phrase [bars 3–5] Zeus hurls thunderbolts. It's angular and angry, with tremendous energy and urgency:

DALLEY   Already at the twenty-fourth bar the second subject is with us. It's cantabile in character, and the tempo needs to be held back. One wants to hear the quicker notes played very singingly. We broaden the melodic triplets a little by anticipating their entrance:

We eventually retake the first tempo at the recurrence of the sixteenth notes; these must always be in tempo.

STEINHARDT   Typical of the almost constant sense of rubato, the up-ward-rising scale [bar 38] rushes headlong towards the bar line—and *then* we wait a moment during the rest. We allow the subsequent lyrical passage just a little more time to sing:

This movement is exceptional in its dramatic disparities of tempo. Generally speaking, as we've played together over the years, we've tried more and more to integrate the parts into the whole. For instance, in the first movement of Schubert's A-minor Quartet we used to play the lyrical first subject [see page 130] in a considerably slower tempo than the subsequent dramatic passage. Each section sounded good in itself, but the overall effect was rather piecemeal. We recorded it that way. But we now take the opening somewhat faster. The contrast in tempos is less drastic and the structure of the whole more cohesive.

DALLEY   One can also follow our quartet's evolution when comparing our present performances with our Beethoven recordings made in the late sixties. One sees that in other groups, too. For instance, with the Budapest Quartet one notes significant differences between recordings of the same piece made at different times.

When comparing your past and present Beethoven performances, I find that your choices of tempo remain fairly consistent for the outer movements and for the slow movements. For instance, the great Adagios of the first two "Razumovsky" quartets and of Opus 132—now as before—unfold unhurriedly, with an enormous sense of breadth. The main differences lie in your approach to some of the middle movements in moderate tempo, particularly from Opus 59 onwards. In general you play these faster than before. One example is the second movement of Opus 59, No. 3, which, I must say, I'm greatly relieved to hear you play in a more flowing tempo.

SOYER   We used to sentimentalize it.

TREE   Why would we have played it slowly? That's what mystifies me. It has a lilt—it's a dance. . .

SOYER   Who knows? We used to do all sorts of things like that.

TREE   We also play the third movement of Opus 59, No. 2 somewhat faster than we used to [see page 65]. Without losing its lyrical, melancholic aspect, we bring a more breathless feeling, and the Trio with its "Thème russe" now falls into place without any change of tempo.

DALLEY   I'm not sure that speeding this up improves it. It may be easier to play, but the whole melodic quality suffers if it's too fast—as does the rustic passage in fortissimo.

TREE   The second movement of Opus 132 is another case in point [see page 33]. We now convey more of its restless, agitated feeling. We used to play it in three beats per bar, but now we feel it in one.

A slower tempo might sound expressive at the beginning, but given the constant repetition of motifs, the movement retains more interest throughout if played in a more rapid tempo.

STEINHARDT   It takes a great deal of courage for a man to write a whole movement with so little variety of material.

DALLEY   It takes more courage to play it.

STEINHARDT   The fourth movement of this quartet—Alla Marcia—is also a little quicker than it used to be.

Although it's forte, it should have a light, buoyant feeling. Once again I appreciate the change; on your recording it's rather stern and heavy—in fact, Bismarckian.

TREE   You can thank Dave for the improvement. Whenever we rehearse it, we can count on his saying that it's a French march, not a German march.

SOYER   American military marches are played at the official tempo of 120. German marches can be slower, but French marches are quicker.

Probably because Napoleon's troops had farther to walk.

DALLEY   They wanted to get home before the wine soured.

TREE   I always feel a tremendous sense of release when playing this march; it doesn't come a moment too soon after the "Heiliger Dankgesang," which is almost a whole work in itself—nearly twenty minutes of music. I think Beethoven wanted that sense of release; the music takes wing.

How do you settle on a tempo should a disagreement arise?

SOYER   There again, what we do now is quite different from what we did in the beginning. We used to have long, long discussions before we'd even play a movement through. Nowadays these questions work themselves out in the playing as we familiarize ourselves with the piece. The tempo may push and pull itself about over a couple of rehearsals. And if we still don't see eye to eye, rather than continue arguing over it we'll try the movement a little faster or slower from one concert to the next.

DALLEY   We once did that in the *same* concert. We had played Beethoven's Opus 59, No. 3 and, coming offstage, three of us proceeded to berate the other for the ridiculously slow tempo he set for the Finale.

TREE   That was me.

DALLEY   And since we had no other available encore, we played the Finale again—and the same violist set a completely different tempo.

SOYER   Equally ridiculous.

STEINHARDT   As fast as humanly possible.

You do generally take this movement faster than one normally hears it.

SOYER   Yes; the metronome indication—the whole note at 84—shows that Beethoven wanted the piece to go very quickly. It's only fairly recently that quartets have begun to play this movement at a vivacious tempo. There was a tradition that it should be taken at a nice, safe, deliberate pace—and, frankly, the effect was deadly.

TREE   Perhaps they wanted to emphasize the serious nature of the fugal material; they didn't want to think of it as a display piece. But I think it *is* a display piece—in the best sense of the term.

STEINHARDT   The tempo is based not only on the brilliant fugal subject [see page 123] but on the second-violin melody that comes towards the end of the movement:

This melody should have an ecstatic quality; its longer note-values won't work in a slow tempo.

TREE   The piece has great bravura, doesn't it? It should raise the roof.

To what extent do you follow Beethoven's metronome markings?

SOYER We regard them as giving a *general* idea of the tempo desired; they tell us something about the basic character of a movement. We try to capture this. But it's immaterial if you play slightly over or under the marking.

TREE Don't forget that it was twenty years after he wrote the Opus 18 quartets that he sat down with that new toy and indicated the markings.

DALLEY His deafness, too, might have led him to conceive a tempo somewhat removed from actual performance.

TREE Even if we were to subscribe wholly to Beethoven's metronome markings, the tempo would change a little from night to night, whatever our intentions. Tempo is something organic.

Beethoven welcomed the metronome as a means of clearing up basic misunderstandings, yet he noted on the manuscript of a song: "100 according to Maelzel—but this should be applied to the first bar only—for feeling also has its own tempo which cannot be expressed by this figure." He shared Rubinstein's view.

SOYER That isn't surprising. Bartók, for instance, would indicate that bar 32 to bar 54 should last 23 seconds. That's pretty exact. However, Bartók's own performances often varied considerably from his markings.

TREE In Shostakovich's performance of his Cello Sonata with Rostropovich the tempos are quite different from the metronome markings.

STEINHARDT We've had similar experiences when playing the works of contemporary composers. For example, Leon Kirchner was rather amused by the seriousness of our approach when we prepared his First String Quartet—the way we examined every one of his markings under a microscope. "No, no," he said, "you must interpret; let your imagination take wing even if it doesn't correspond to what's on the printed page."

As Villa-Lobos used to say, "The heart is the metronome of life."

DALLEY I think we'd all agree to that.

Would anyone like to comment on Rudolf Kolisch's theory that throughout all of

Beethoven's works, basic correlations can be drawn between character types and tempos? ★

STEINHARDT Kolisch's speculations are interesting and very controversial. One can disagree, but they'll stimulate three-quarters of an hour of conversation. We ourselves have difficulty conceiving musical ideas in terms of theoretical abstractions. We are pragmatic players. We roll up our sleeves and judge something on its own merits without making learned comparisons.

SOYER Kolisch tied things up into neat packages. Since, for instance, the opening of the G-major Piano Concerto and the second subject of the first movement of the "Archduke" Trio have certain similarities of configuration and rhythm, they're supposed to be played in the same tempo. He once gave a famous lecture on this subject. Otto Klemperer, who was in the audience, suddenly stood up, stopping the lecture dead in the middle. "Kolisch," he said in a loud voice. "Yes, Dr. Klemperer?" "Excuse me, but where is the bathroom?"

* Rudolf Kolisch, "Tempo and Character in Beethoven's Music," *Musical Quarterly,* Vol. 29, Nos. 2 and 3 (1943).

FOUR VOICES

David Soyer

At what moment did you feel you were destined to become a cellist?

SOYER   Almost immediately upon beginning. I had no doubt about it. I started when I was eleven, which is a little late for a string player, though not so very late for a cellist. I had already studied the piano for a couple of years. My first teacher was Emmet Sargeant, a member of the Philadelphia Orchestra, who gave me a sense of what the cello is about and an attitude of fearlessness in approaching it. He was very supportive, and I progressed rapidly. Although my parents weren't musicians, they appreciated what I was doing. My sister, a pianist—she now teaches in New York—was very helpful to me. When I was thirteen we moved from Philadelphia to New York. At that time the New York Philharmonic offered scholarships which entitled the winners to study with first-desk players in the orchestra and take courses in chamber music and theory. I received this scholarship and studied for a year with Joseph Emonts, who was assistant first cellist to Alfred Wallenstein— Toscanini then being the orchestra's conductor. I studied harmony with Emmet Sargeant's brother Winthrop, who became a well-known music critic.

My next teacher was Diran Alexanian, who had been Casals's assistant at the Ecole Normale de Musique in Paris before coming to America. I was then fourteen, and I remained with him for four years. Alexanian was a truly remarkable man. He had an amazing background, having been a student of Henri Bergson in philosophy and having studied chamber music with Brahms. He had known Debussy, Ravel, Saint-Saëns, and many other outstanding musicians and had been part of the circle of intellectuals that included Cocteau and Diaghilev. He could play almost any opera score on the piano from memory. His well-known cello manual was endorsed by Casals. Among his students were Emanuel Feuermann, Mischa Schneider, Antonio Janigro, and Bernard Greenhouse. As a teacher he was severe and dogmatic—a rather frightening figure for a young musician—but I survived it.

Alexanian had specific ideas about cello playing and interpretation and brooked no deviation. While teaching a concerto he would often say, "Now go to the piano and play the orchestra part"—and we had to be prepared for this; he expected his students to have made a harmonic analysis of the piece. For example, in the slow movement of the Dvořák Concerto he might ask what influence a given chord has on the cello line. Alexanian had the rare ability to teach a student how to learn a work. I try to carry on this approach in my own teaching. For instance, how does one go about studying a Bach suite, in which there are no dynamic or tempo markings? One should first identify the melodic, harmonic, and rhythmic elements. Where are the melodic arcs? Where are the breaks in the line which create apostrophes in the phrasing? Where are modulations, dissonances, and other points of emphasis in the underlying harmony? What is the basic character of the piece? Does it have a dance lilt, and if so, to what extent should that be stressed? How do all these factors help determine the tempo?

Alexanian also taught us how to practice. Oh yes, one puts one's finger down here and the bow there—but all that can be quite mechanical. It's pointless to do something over and over again if you're repeating the same mistake; all you're doing is practicing the mistake and ingraining it. Practicing well is virtually an art in itself—the art of achieving economy of time and means. Alexanian would approach a problem in the following manner: "That's not good. What's not good about it? What should it be? How do you do it?" One learned to use one's ears and one's brain to analyze every difficulty.

I do differ from Alexanian, however, in my own teaching when it comes to respecting differing viewpoints with regard to interpretation or even technique. If a student's way is legitimate in its own right, I'll accept it. If, on the other hand, I think that he or she is eventually going to run into trouble, I'll advise changes. Since people are so different from one another—with different abilities and different physical characteristics—I have no set method of teaching. I try to work with a student's strengths and correct the weaknesses.

When I left Alexanian I went to Emanuel Feuermann; it was then about a year before his death.

What was your estimation of his playing?

SOYER   He was an extraordinary artist. His tragic death at thirty-nine deprived him of the chance to reach his full maturity as a musician. But he had incredible potential. We have the legacy of his recordings, but none of them does him complete justice.

What sort of man was he?

SOYER   On the surface he could be rather flippant. He was rough on his students; his satire could be devastating. He had some cute little tricks such as hitting a student on the head with his bow and then laughing. On more than one occasion I was rapped smartly on the skull. But in the main I got along with him.

Do you use that technique with your own students?

SOYER   I haven't tried it yet. I used to scream and yell at them, until I discovered that they weren't learning much but just crying. So I gave that up.

Interestingly enough, I often learned more from Feuermann in our discussions after the lessons than during them. He had many valuable pragmatic suggestions to make, derived from his experience on the concert platform. For example, when I got to know Casals some years later, one of the things he used to say was, "I relax my hand after striking every note." Well, Feuermann had also spoken of this, in a different way. As he put it, "Every note has its own life." They were both referring to the idea that the very beginning of a note is the critical point of intensity. There should be an almost instantaneous sequence of percussion, vibrato, and relaxation. It might be compared to the throwing of a knife into the floor and observing its initial impact and quivering. Feuermann's left-hand technique was fairly similar to that of Casals—the same attention to articulation, the same principle of shifting on semitones when possible. But he was less prone to use extensions and made somewhat more frequent use of glissandos. Alexanian had been very strict in that regard; you weren't allowed to make a glissando unless you had five excellent reasons for doing so. When I came to Feuermann I was a pretty brash kid, so I asked, "Why do you slide so much?" As he was a pretty brash guy, he didn't mind that. "I slide," he said, "because I'm not playing the clarinet; I'm playing the cello. When I put my fingers down I'm not just covering holes. The slides give a sense of fluency and a vocal quality. Try singing a phrase and not sliding and see how far you get. It's a perfectly natural way of playing." And when you think about it, of course it is. Some people took exception to his taste in this regard, but, in the main, what he did was very attractive.

Feuermann's playing was, I think, greatly influenced by his association with Heifetz; he tried to carry over something of Heifetz's style to cello playing. "Think of a good bow arm," he would say. "It will normally not be that of a cellist but of a violinist. Let's try to do what the violinists do." Feuermann's bow arm was much, much better than Alexanian's. It was far more relaxed and flexible, yet the wrist remained relatively quiet; there wasn't all of the paint brushing with the wrist that many French cellists favor. If when changing the bow you also have to move your hand, lose and regain the grip of the bow on the string, all in one instant, the sound can be interrupted. Since Feuermann's hand remained supple, it reacted a little as a result of a change of bow direction, but the motion originated from the arm rather than the wrist. Casals's wrist motion was, if anything, quieter yet.

There followed a period of three and a half years spent playing the euphonium in the Navy band in Washington. This turned out to be a surprisingly creative time in my development. I was able to appraise my past musical experiences in retrospect, and I also had the opportunity to be in contact with many outstanding musicians, such as Bernard Greenhouse and Oscar Shumsky, who were fellow band members. Luckily, we also had a chance to play our stringed instruments in an orchestra. In keeping with Feuermann's advice about violinists, I consulted Oscar Shumsky about bowing. Oscar is a great violinist—a dedicated musician of tremendous integrity. His bow arm is marvelous, and his advice proved most helpful. Under Alexanian's influence I had gripped the bow quite tightly, my fingers being straight with virtually no play in them. Oscar showed me how to hold the bow in a more relaxed way and how to change the balance of the hand as the bow moves from the frog to the point and back again. In fact, the natural weight of the bow is virtually enough in itself to provide adequate strength at the frog, with very little hand pressure needed. Oscar also recommended bow exercises that took one through every possible combination of slurred and detached notes. I try to get my students to do this. It's a nasty sort of thing, but most beneficial.

I can't sufficiently emphasize the importance of developing the bow arm. Mastery of the bow is the key to freedom in interpretation. A string player should have sufficient control to be able to change the bow without breaking the continuity of the phrase, and to make a crescendo or diminuendo with equal ease on an up- or a down-bow. I must confess that I'm not very disciplined when it comes to following prearranged bowings. I don't always remember what bowings I've decided on, because I don't mark my score very much unless it's critical that our bowing be concerted. When I'm involved in the music and shaping the line I'm sometimes not even conscious of whether I'm playing up- or down-bow. Casals rarely prescribed a bowing as such. It was always a question of phrasing, and of being careful not to destroy it with what you do with the bow. "Don't be a prisoner of the bow," he would say. If you can play more freely and find the sound you want by changing the bow, change it by all means.

I've already referred to another musician who influenced me strongly: Frank Miller, at that time solo cellist of the NBC Symphony. Although I wasn't a regular member of the orchestra, I played with it occasionally and also had the opportunity to sit next to Frank when we did certain radio shows. I admired him immensely. He was a wonderful cellist—the best first cellist of an orchestra I've ever known from the standpoint of leading ability, assurance, and strength. And when he had solos to play they were beautiful. He was a very kind and sweet man. Toscanini had great confidence in him. There's a story which, though Frank denied it, I still believe to be true. Guest conductors sometimes took over the NBC Symphony, and Frank wasn't always happy with their interpretations. On occasion when he found the tempo to be unduly fast, he would begin to pull back. With his tremendous strength he would bring the cello and bass sections along with him; the whole bottom of the orchestra would put the brakes on, and the tempo would slow down.

Do you sometimes do that in the Guarneri String Quartet?

SOYER   I wouldn't admit to it publicly. Let's just say that Frank Miller had an influence on me in certain respects.

What was it like to play under Toscanini?

SOYER   It was, of course, a memorable experience. A focal point of energy existed on the podium—a white-hot intensity, vital, concise, rhythmically concentrated. His stick technique was absolutely simple and clear. You always knew what was being said with the baton. His upbeat was so precise and conveyed the mood and tempo with such clarity that sometimes he wouldn't even need to give a downbeat. When he flew into rages—tearing up his jacket or destroying his score (only if it could readily be replaced)—it was more in anger with himself than with anyone else. He was like a teacher who feels, "My students aren't doing well and it's my fault." The reins were always tightly held, and I felt that at times this produced a certain restraint in the actual sonority. Of course, Toscanini wasn't looking for the luscious richness of, say, the Philadelphia Orchestra under Stokowski. One sometimes hears Toscanini described as inflexible in his approach to tempo, but I rarely found that to be true. He had a wonderful lyric sense and was constantly urging the orchestra to sing. He knew how to make a melody sound full and free without disturbing the overall rhythmic proportions.

In this respect he was like Casals, who based his rubato on the principle of "fantasy—but with order."

SOYER   Yes. And Casals, like Toscanini, had a transcendental way of making music. I first met him in Marlboro in 1962; I played for him then and on many subsequent occasions. If I had to epitomize his attitude towards music in a single word, it would be "love." He dared to trust his intuition, and he had enormous courage. Many musicians are concerned with the opinions of others; their playing has to be pretty, smooth, and luscious at all times, no matter what the music calls for. But Casals would interpret a work just as he thought it should be, traditions and the public's preconceived attitudes notwithstanding. If he felt a passage should be played without vibrato, he would play it that way. His music making transcended any personal consideration. One didn't think of Pablo Casals; one heard only the essence of the music. It was nonetheless an individual way of playing, unique to him. No one could copy him. Some of his students have tried, but no one has succeeded. He brought the full force of his integrity to every work he played. When you listen to his recording of the Rubinstein Melody in F, you believe at that moment that it's one of the most beautiful pieces of music ever written.

Marlboro was in itself a decisive experience for me, as I know it has also been for my colleagues in the quartet. My first weeks there were a complete mystery to me. It seemed an amorphous organization, and I wondered how it managed to function so well. But I adored it. I met Rudolf Serkin at that time, and we've since become close friends. Michael Tree and I played together for a while in the Marlboro Trio; and, of course, in 1964 our quartet was formed.

When had you first started to play chamber music?

SOYER   Almost as soon as I began to play the cello. I remember discovering my sister's music for the Brahms Piano Quintet. "Good God," I thought, "here's a work for five instruments!" I had my first experience playing string quartets when I was thirteen, as part of the New York Philharmonic scholarship program. It wasn't an auspicious beginning. We sat down to play Haydn's "Quinten" Quartet. As I could hardly sight-read at all, I was completely lost after three bars. The other players, all of whom were two or three years older than I, were quite disgusted and called for a replacement, who turned out to be Claus Adam, then a huge fellow of seventeen or eighteen. I improved my reading by playing chamber music whenever I could, and I eventually found myself dedicated to it. I later played in the Bach Aria Group and in various string quartets: the Guilet, the American, the Musical Arts, and the New Music.

What would you advise a young cellist to look out for in quartet playing?

SOYER   Above all that the cello should fulfill the dual roles of *base* and *bass*. In the role of *base* the cellist has to assure the foundation of the ensemble. There must be sufficient sense of presence and substance of sound to provide a point of stability. In the role of *bass* the cellist must give life to the harmonic structure. Sensitivity to harmonic motion will have a crucial influence on the timing and placement of notes, degrees of emphasis, and choices in intonation.

The cello is also often called upon to act as rhythmic monitor of the quartet—setting the pulse, articulating points of rhythmic stress, conveying a sense of rhythmic direction. This requires not only an intellectual but an instinctive knowledge of what rhythm really is.

It was very helpful for me to have had the experience playing the continuo in the Bach Aria Group. Bach's bass parts have a continual vitality—not only harmonically but rhythmically and melodically as well. In the cantatas the bass is often built on characteristic motifs meant to depict the imagery of the text: waves, steadfastness, descent into the grave, etc. Playing this music helps one develop a feeling for the character and shaping of the bass line in every phrase.

Would you say that the cello and the first violin create a kind of structure for the quartet? Mozart, for instance, would first sketch the melody and the bass line, filling in the inner voices at a later stage. Is that kind of thinking relevant to quartet playing?

SOYER   Yes, indeed. I wish young cellists would keep that in mind. They're almost always too retiring when playing quartets. I constantly find myself urging them to play with greater vitality than they think called for. This principle applies to the whole repertoire, from Haydn to Bartók.

Schubert's C-major Quintet is an interesting case in point. In this work Schubert generally gives the role of lyric tenor to the first cello and the true bass to the second cello. But young players taking the second part often think, "I'm just in a subsidiary role and shouldn't get in anyone's way." They usually practice the thirty-second-note figures in the latter part of the slow movement and play them well while neglecting everything else, including the pizzicato at the beginning of the movement, which should be an equal partner to the first-violin figure. In fact, the performance of the work can stand or fall on the execution of the second cello part. There's a world of difference when the second cellist approaches his part with initiative and creativity.

The biggest trap for a cellist is to look at a series of eighth notes in, say, a Haydn or a Mozart quartet and consider them easy, if not downright boring. A series of notes which appear to be similar to one another on paper need not necessarily sound equal; they may change direction or function at any time. And many Haydn quartets are surely far from easy. From Opus 17 onwards his cello writing begins to be rather complex. Composers were often influenced by the players they knew. The virtuoso cellists Joseph Weigl and Anton Kraft were at different times members of the orchestra at Esterháza. Haydn undoubtedly had them in mind when writing his concertos and some of the rather elaborate cello parts in his quartets and symphonies.

With Mozart the cello writing—always interesting and often contrapuntal—is mostly integrated into the texture, avoiding solo display. The exceptions are the three quartets dedicated to the king of Prussia, Friedrich Wilhelm, who was an amateur cellist. In these works the cello often plays the melody in the upper register, the viola meanwhile taking over the role of bass. The voicing is unusual, the sonority being lighter-weight and more transparent than in other Mozart quartets—and the cello parts are very difficult.

Having been taught by one of the Duport brothers, the king must have played reasonably well.

SOYER   At least he owned a good instrument: the "Stuart" Strad.

Your Guarneri cello is greatly admired. When did you acquire it?

SOYER   I came across it forty-five years ago, when I was a student. It was love at first sight, but I only had about two and a half dollars to my name, and the instrument was utterly beyond my reach. I eventually acquired a fine Montagnana but kept an eye on the Guarneri. Eighteen years ago it came up for sale again, and I bought it. It was built in 1669 by Andrea Guarneri, the first instrument maker in the family. He didn't make many cellos—ten or fifteen at most. This may possibly be the finest example of his work—so the dealers say. The bass is very strong; it's a baritone rather than a tenor. The sound is dark yet robust.

Didn't you play for some time on Casals's instrument?

SOYER   Yes. I first looked after his Bergonzi-Goffriller in New York when he found that the climate in Puerto Rico was too humid for it. It was a sacrifice for him to part with the instrument he had played daily for fifty years. After his death his wife, Marta, wanted the instrument to be played and suggested that I borrow it. I kept it for two years and enjoyed it very much. Its personality is so distinctive, however, that I didn't find it to be an ideal instrument for the quartet. It's clear and brilliant, but there's more to it than that. It has a special voice—penetrating, pungent—which one associated with Casals. As I wasn't using it often, I agreed to Marta's suggestion that it be lent to a young Catalan cellist who was here on tour and needed a fine instrument. And the cello is now back in Marta's custody. I was amused when Casals would say that he preferred not to play on a Strad because he didn't want a cello with too specific a personality of its own. In fact, his Bergonzi-Goffriller had a far more personal sound than most Strads—but it was, of course, just the sound that Casals liked.

We've already stressed the fact that quartet instruments have really to be of solo quality. This is of special importance for the cello, which by its very nature is already at a certain disadvantage. Owing to the thickness of its strings it doesn't respond as readily as do the higher-voiced instruments; the lower strings in particular have greater resistance. However, by various technical means one can compensate for this inequality. Certain figures will often speak better if played nearer the frog and off the string; this especially applies to rapid, detached notes. It's also sometimes not advisable to try to play as many notes on one bow as will a violinist. However, I do believe that a cellist with a good bow arm can do almost anything that a violinist can, with hardly any exceptions. The song "One Can't Do That on the Cello" doesn't mean much anymore.

Good articulation with the left hand is indispensable if the strings are to be made to speak immediately. Left-hand pizzicato in descending passages at the moment the finger leaves the string is also a valuable aid. That was typical of the Casals and Feuermann school.

I note that you sometimes enhance the articulation by means of a simultaneous action of right and left hands.

SOYER   Yes, they join together to set the string in motion. I do that often when I want a clear beginning, even in lyrical passages. Take, for instance, the opening of Beethoven's Opus 59, No. 1. At the very instant the bow touches the string, the finger strikes it vibrantly:

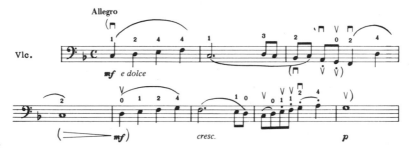

As this is one of the most notable cello passages in the quartet literature, it might be interesting to look at it in detail. How do you approach the interpretation of these eight bars?

SOYER   I think it's important that the theme be heard in its long line; I take care that there's no real breath before the end of the fourth bar.

Do you conceive the rhythmic pulsation as alla breve?

SOYER   Not in the sense that I divide the bars into strong and weak beats—the first and third quarters being strong, for example. I don't really believe in that. Arnold gives more attention to this sort of thing than I do. I agree that there *are* strong beats and weak beats, but they don't follow academic rules. In this case one could more readily think of the phrase as being in one big beat per bar. In Opus 131 Beethoven has marked "Ritmo di quattro battute," which in its context means "rhythm of four bars." It's clear that he was aware of this question of the grouping of several bars together.

Do you treat the C's that begin the first, second, and fourth bars differently?

SOYER   I would probably give a little more intensity to each one in turn. There seems to be a natural nuance of rise and fall from the second half of the third bar into the fourth bar; the whole-note C would then taper off, but only with a diminuendo, not with a break. Since the next phrase comes at a higher level, I would begin the fifth bar with a shade more tone than the first bar. I use the open D string here. Not only is the fingering less awkward, but I also prefer the open sonority. In the very first bar I shift on the half step, as Casals often would, using a 4–4 fingering from E to F. One doesn't want the F to be too high, and this fingering helps to control it. The F may, however, have a wolf; if so, it can be rather treacherous. Should I feel the need for greater solidity, I might change the fingering to 3–4 on the E–F. Another way to deal with the wolf is to squeeze the cello with your knees. That usually gets it under control.

That's the last thing in the world one would think of when hearing you play such a noble theme!

SOYER   Such is a cellist's lot: just a little squeeze for that moment—not hard enough to crack the instrument, of course—and then you can let go.

One has to be careful to save the bow in the second bar so that the two detached notes in the third bar don't come out too close to the frog and get rather heavy as a result. On the other hand, if they're too far away from the frog they'll be difficult to control. Sometimes I play the bowing just as marked in the score, and sometimes I take a separate down-bow for the two slurred notes at the beginning of the third bar.

Taking another solo passage—the beginning of the second movement of Beethoven's Opus 95—one feels an immediate sense of presence in the way you play each note:

SOYER   Here again I apply the principle of simultaneous right- and left-hand articulation. The sonority shouldn't be too timid; the marking is "mezza voce," not "sotto voce"; a kind of *mp/mf* is implied. I play all the dotted eighths down-bow, using about half of the bow for each stroke. One can think of the eighth as being the length of the note and the dot as being the ring as the bow leaves the string; that seems to work quite well. Retaking the bow helps to ensure clear enunciation. The initial vibrato is very rapid and then tapers off; it's as if each note were sounded in turn by a tuning fork. Setting just the right tempo is, of course, crucial. I find that it helps in this respect to think of the fugue subject that comes later in the movement [bar 35].

When the motif appears in bar 65 I don't retake the bow but play down/up as it comes, at the point, so as not to disturb the pianissimo. I nonetheless maintain clear articulation.

As I've said before, the Quartet always treats Beethoven's pianissimo passages with special care. A sense of mystery is evoked here.

SOYER It's wonderfully orchestrated, isn't it? The three upper voices, suspended high above the cello, give a crystalline quality. At the fourth bar, where a suspension occurs in the other voices, I give a slight emphasis to the B natural and then make a diminuendo. The same pattern applies to the subsequent phrase. This is a typical example of how the bass can subtly pinpoint moments of harmonic intensity.

A striking example of where you bring a revelatory, dramatic presence to an often unadventuresome-sounding bass figure is the pizzicato used throughout the second movement of Beethoven's Opus 59, No. 3:

SOYER   These are far more than accompanying, subsidiary figures. Beethoven sets the whole nocturnal, mysterious dance in this frame. I have a subjective image here. I hear in these repeated pizzicato bass notes the tolling of a bell—a calling to judgment, a funeral knell. Luckily, the great length of the cello strings makes it really possible for one to interpret the pizzicato, to control and shape it to a far greater degree than would be possible on a violin. In the fifth and sixth bars one can make a very strong crescendo into the forte. These notes should be declaimed; an increase in vibrato will help. One has to be careful to pull the string not upwards but to the side—as a guitarist would—so that there's no danger of the string hitting the fingerboard with a snapping sound. It's good to play down towards the rosin, near the end of the fingerboard, so that you get quite a bit of resistance from the string.

Before the recapitulation, where the pizzicato subsides to pp, *you play without any vibrato at all; then comes the shock of the forte:*

I'm reminded of Arthur Nikisch's classic description of the quiet trumpet notes towards the end of the second movement of Beethoven's Seventh Symphony: "It's as if someone were knocking on my coffin."

SOYER   I'll accept the imagery; there's no question of this music's very serious nature.

You create such a sinister atmosphere with the pizzicatos in this movement that I can only take comfort in the knowledge that you are in fact a most affable person. I have to remind myself, "He's really gentle as a lamb."

SOYER   Well, that proves my point that cellists shouldn't despair when confronted with pages of ordinary-looking bass notes. We have the power to transform ourselves from lambs into wolves, and back into lambs again.

Michael Tree

It's interesting to note that a number of great composers took particular pleasure in playing the viola.

TREE   Mozart's affection for the instrument is well documented. He played it in quartets in which the violin parts were taken by Haydn and Dittersdorf. I wouldn't have minded being there! Beethoven, too, played the viola; he owned a lovely instrument which we've seen in his house in Bonn. In family musical gatherings Schubert normally took the viola part, and he also led the viola section in an orchestra formed of friends and colleagues.

Bach's preference for the viola is described by his first biographer, Forkel: "With this instrument he was, as it were, in the center of the harmony, where he could hear and enjoy to the utmost what was going on on both sides of him."★

TREE   I congratulate all these masters on their good taste. Indeed, nothing is more satisfying than hearing the sounds around you in every register—responding to them and blending with them. We violists don't play as many melodies as the first violin does, but that's not all there is to music. Some composers—Mendelssohn among them—wrote such fine inner voices that they're as pleasurable to play as the outer voices. Schubert, for instance, had such an all-pervading melodic gift that some of his inner voices could be extracted as melodies in themselves. When he alternates between major and minor—which he so loves to do—it's often the viola that lowers or raises the third of the chord and brings about that sudden, heartbreaking change of mood. I try to impress on young quartet players the idea that there's really no such thing as an "accompaniment"; the inner voices always play a crucial role in terms of sensitivity and beauty of sound within the ensemble. We can't just play dry eighth notes under a melody. In fact, if a so-called accompaniment figure is played in a wooden manner, the melody itself will sound less beautiful.

★ J. N. Forkel, *Über J. S. Bachs Leben, Kunst und Kunstwerke* (Leipzig, 1802).

Prior to joining the quartet, you had already established a career as a solo violinist. Was it difficult to make the adjustment to quartet playing?

TREE   The truth is that I always enjoyed playing quartets, even as a child. Every week we had chamber-music sessions in our home; sometimes two or three quartets would be playing simultaneously in various rooms. A fair sprinkling of professional musicians participated, but the main impetus for these gatherings came from amateur players, and performing with them provided some of my most meaningful encounters with the quartet repertoire. Many years later I was to experience chamber music on quite another level at the Marlboro Festival. Marlboro offers young musicians the invaluable opportunity to play as colleagues alongside outstanding and highly experienced artists. It was marvelous as a young man to find myself playing in ensembles with such people as Rudolf Serkin, Felix Galimir, and members of the Budapest Quartet. Although we hadn't yet formed our quartet, Arnold, John, Dave, and I played together a great deal, too. Naturally, when questions arose about interpretation, we young players would normally defer to our more experienced colleagues. But I do remember that we once almost shocked the pants off of Mischa Schneider when, in the Mendelssohn Octet, we pulled a few stunts that he hadn't heard before; he was most amused and very encouraging. Marlboro was, in fact, the creative matrix from which our quartet was born. Of course, Arnold, John, and I had already known each other from Curtis.

Which I understand you entered at an early age.

TREE   Yes, when I was twelve. Coincidentally, it was the violist William Primrose who had heard me play and recommended that I continue my violin studies at Curtis.

At what age did you begin to play the violin?

TREE   When I was five. I was fortunate in having in my father, Samuel Applebaum, a fine violinist with a great deal of experience teaching youngsters. He looked after my playing day by day, sometimes for only a few minutes at a time, fitting me in between his regular students. It wasn't until I went to Curtis that I had a formal violin lesson in the conventional sense, where I was required to be in a particular room at a given time to spend an hour with a teacher. But it was an advantage to me as a child to have my father's supervision in small doses rather than having only one lesson a week and then being left to my own devices. As a result of my father's teaching I was sufficiently well equipped at the age of twelve to enter Curtis and begin to direct my attention towards matters of interpretation.

It was an exciting new life. As we lived in Newark, my mother and I would spend part of the week in Philadelphia and return home for long weekends. It was then just after the war, and a lot of veterans were returning to Curtis. I found myself rubbing shoulders with people in their twenties. In addition to instrumental studies the curriculum included harmony, counterpoint, the history of music, even languages. And, of course, the state insisted that all students under sixteen have tutoring in academic subjects.

Wasn't it difficult when taking the theoretical courses to keep up with the older students?

TREE   I just managed—with a great deal of struggle and poor marks. But the faculty at Curtis has always been understanding and has shown personal interest in the students. And now they have a preparatory division that's specially set up for young players.

During my first year I studied with Lea Luboshutz; after her retirement I went on to work with Efrem Zimbalist for another ten years. I also had coaching with Veda Reynolds, an outstanding violinist and a remarkable quartet player. She saw to it that I did my instrumental homework. I went through the full training of the Russian school of violin playing, studying virtually the whole étude literature and every nineteenth-century virtuoso concerto, some rarely heard today.

John Dalley also studied with Zimbalist. We agree that he was a marvelous pedagogue. His outlook was very experimental, particularly in regard to fingering. He believed—as Szigeti did—that the hand should creep around the fingerboard, as it were, taking in more than one position at a time, thus avoiding a lot of unnecessary shifting and glissandos. Zimbalist's style of playing was quite unlike that of some of the other Leopold Auer students. It was more reserved; his use of vibrato was more discreet. He was renowned for his bow arm; he used to astonish us with his control. It was said that he could sustain a given note or phrase beautifully on a single bow longer than anyone else. When it came to interpretation he never imposed his will; he hoped that we would strike out and find our own ways—though when he felt something was played unstylistically he could, in his own quiet way, make his opinion known very forcefully. He produced many fine students, most of whom played quite differently not only from him but also from each other, and I think this speaks well for his teaching.

When did you take up the viola?

TREE   I played it a little at Curtis. And when I went to Marlboro I expressed interest in doing *some* viola playing, little realizing what this was soon to lead to. It was a pivotal evening in my life when Rudolf Serkin asked me to play both the violin and the viola in a chamber-music concert at the Metropolitan Museum in New York, lending me for the occasion a beautiful Guadagnini viola that had belonged to Adolf Busch. I was concerned about switching rapidly from one instrument to the other but was assured that there would be plenty of time between pieces. Well, as luck would have it, the program was arranged in such a way that I barely had time to put down one instrument and snatch up the other. My first public appearance as a violist was thus a sort of baptism of fire. There are a number of outstanding violinists—Jaime Laredo, Oscar Shumsky, Pinchas Zukerman, and others—who play both instruments and alternate between them on the same evening. I do that too on occasion—not in the quartet but when giving sonata recitals. I think it's interesting for the public to hear both instruments played at the same concert.

There's a rumor that a coin was tossed to decide who would play the viola in the Guarneri String Quartet.

TREE   I don't know how that story got started. We've heard it a hundred times. There isn't a grain of truth in it; I was *delighted* to play the viola.

What sort of color do you prefer in a viola sound? Primrose favored a mezzo-soprano timbre, Tertis a contralto.

TREE   Having been trained as a violinist, my thoughts were always focused on the upper register, with its sweet soprano quality. But the more I played the viola, the more my perception of its sonority changed; I began thinking in increasingly darker hues. I've finally become enamored of the idea of producing a deep, rich, "chocolaty" sound. The viola may even have brought out another side of my nature. I feel rather like a singer who's developed a new register—a Don Ottavio who can now take on the role of Don Giovanni. Playing the viola influences not only your tone production but your way of looking at music, your way of playing a phrase. I don't know how to explain that in logical terms, but I suspect that a given phrase would be played somewhat differently on the viola than on the violin even if the notes were in a similar context— just as a phrase played in the upper register of the piano might be inflected somewhat differently if it were played two octaves lower. It's interesting to note that when Bartók set about writing his Viola Concerto he asked William Primrose to play the viola for him at length so that he could immerse himself thoroughly in the sound of the instrument. Mind you, he had already composed all of those wonderful quartets, which show how well he understood stringed instruments. Afterwards he told Primrose how deeply struck he was by the viola's strongly masculine quality. That may not go down well today with the women's liberation movement. But certainly in Mozart's Sinfonia Concertante the viola does take on a deep, masculine timbre, as opposed to the comparative sweetness and lightness of the violin; it's like a duet in an opera.

I would, in any case, advocate a darker-sounding viola for quartet use. It's important that the instrument have a powerful C string; this is particularly useful for blending with the cello. Most violas of a predominantly treble timbre, no matter how beautiful the quality, have some difficulty when it comes to bringing out the low notes. To have a strong lower register usually means playing on a large instrument. This is a disadvantage to some players; a certain amount of extra work is involved in negotiating the upper positions. But I think it's worth the effort. The concerto and sonata repertoires, however, make somewhat different demands; the same sort of blend isn't necessary, and the purely gymnastic requirements may be greater. For such works it might be advantageous to play on a smaller instrument. I myself sometimes borrow smaller instruments for such occasions.

Doesn't one's physical makeup play a major role in determining the best size of the instrument?

TREE Certainly, though I assume that anybody playing the viola will be able to negotiate an instrument of at least sixteen inches (the length of the back, not including the neck and scroll) without risk of straining the hand.

Would you describe your own instrument?

TREE   When the quartet started out I didn't even own a viola. For the first few years I was slumming, borrowing anything I could get my hands on, and people were very kindly making instruments available to me. I must have played on four or five different violas in concerts and recordings. I owe special thanks to Boris Kroyt for the use of a beautiful Deconet viola which he lent me for some time. For the last ten years or so, however, I've been playing an instrument from 1750 made by Domenico Busan, a contemporary of other masters of the Venetian school such as Goffriller, Seraphin, and Montagnana. It's an extremely large instrument—17 inches long and rather broad shouldered. I have to work a little harder to get around it, but it has a wonderfully clear sound and a rather dark quality as well. This particular instrument was for many years in the Hungarian String Quartet. Interestingly, it was originally a full inch and a half longer. Before Mozart, the technical demands made upon viola players were less rigorous, and it was feasible to play such big instruments. In the course of time, my viola was cut down by three-quarters of an inch at either end.

Isn't it difficult to find a fine viola, especially if it proves awkward to play on a large instrument?

TREE   It's easier than it used to be. The school of stringed-instrument making is as healthy today as it's ever been. I suspect that some of our present-day craftsmen will be remembered as the Stradivari, Amati, and Guarneri of our age. Most are quite young and are experimental in a truly creative sense.

At what stage in their instrumental development should violin students change over to the viola?

TREE   That situation has altered considerably over the years. It used to be the case that most players only turned to the viola after completing a full training as violinists. But nowadays more and more students are taking up the instrument as soon as their hand is large enough to accommodate it. Early in life they decide they want to play the viola, and they already turn to it in their adolescent years.

Having mastered both instruments, what do you consider to be some of the main differences between viola and violin technique?

TREE   Oh, that's a big one! It's not merely a question of the viola sounding a fifth lower and requiring larger spaces between intervals; it's a
question of hearing in a fundamentally different way and wanting to
produce a sound that's truly characteristic of the viola. This involves a
difference in approach for both the right and the left hand. In general, as
I've already mentioned, the vibrato should be wider and somewhat
slower. But this varies to some extent, owing to the fact that the viola is
in a pivotal position. If, for example, I'm playing an accompaniment
figure in thirds with the second violin, I'll reduce the width of my vibrato so as to blend with the higher-voiced instrument. But if I'm shar-
ing a figure with the cello, the vibrato may need to be somewhat wider.
After a while these reactions become almost instinctive. The bow also
requires a certain amount of adjustment. For one thing, we have to think
a little bit more like cellists in our way of drawing or coaxing the tone.
We have to get more "into the string," more into the core of the sound,
and this sometimes requires a slightly greater vertical bow pressure. But
here one must use discretion; the viola bow is thicker and heavier than a
violin bow, as well as being somewhat shorter, and too heavy a stroke
can crush the sound. Rapid strokes which can be played on the violin
with a lot of bow might sound rather glassy or inarticulate on the viola
because of our longer, thicker strings. We'll therefore use less bow and,
like a cellist, tend to play such strokes a little closer to the frog and
somewhat off the string to get the sort of bite that will set the string
immediately in vibration. Articulation is a crucial factor on the viola,
and one must often go to considerable lengths to obtain it—far beyond
what is ordinarily necessary on the violin.

In your performance last night of Dvořák's E-flat-major Quartet [Opus 51] I
noticed how remarkably clearly the viola passages projected.

TREE   Projection is the word, and if I seem somewhat obsessed with it,
I have good reason. In the midst of a thick quartet-texture many viola
passages can be all but lost to the ear. This applies to details which can
easily be overlooked. I could cite several instances from the Finale of the
Dvořák quartet. Take the viola's little interpolation of sixteenth notes at
the end of the opening theme [bar 8]—a motif played just before by the
two violins but which I now have all by myself, and which comes on
the heels of a forte chord:

The normal thing to do, since I'm in first position, would be to stay there and play an open G. I've found, however, that the figure projects far better if I take the trouble to shift to the C string for the last three notes. I do this for two reasons: first of all, the C string is just plain louder, and second of all, I can play with greater force and abandon because there's no string farther to the left of the C string. If I were to stay on the G string, I'd have to be a bit careful not to touch the C string and also not to let the open string twang or alter in pitch.

Or take the passage beginning in bar 60:

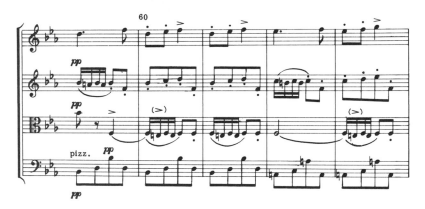

The sixteenth notes coming off of the suspension will sound muddled if the first note isn't accented; a slight rearticulation of the bow is needed. In all the sixteenth-note figures which run through this movement it's crucial that the left hand be extremely strong. The worst enemy of clarity is a mushy left hand. John has already pointed out that in soft legato passages it's doubly important for the left hand to be decisive. I like to hear the thud of the finger when it hits the fingerboard; I listen for that in my own playing, and I'm even more demanding when it comes to listening to my students.

The viola takes the main theme of the Dvořák Finale at different times, and I change the bowing according to the context. This may seem self-indulgent; but, given all its repetitions, the theme, I think, benefits when there's some variety in its treatment. At bar 26 I take the dynamic up to *mp* and divide the legato slur to have a little more weight of sound:

Near the end of the movement the theme is given to the viola [bar 379], just after a triumphant climax in fortissimo. The diminuendo doesn't even begin until the middle of my phrase. So in order to let the theme speak properly and give it sufficient emphasis, I'll play the sixteenths with separate bows, excepting two notes, which I slur so that I come out at bar 380 on an up-bow, giving the B flat a little lift. For the last six notes of the theme I'll again go over to the C string for added strength:

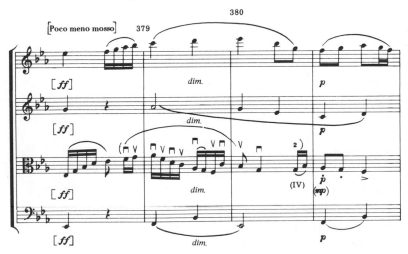

In the echo to this statement [bar 383] I revert to a more legato bowing because there's no longer a balance problem and the character is more singing. Then, beginning at bar 386, we have four bars in a row of the same motif. I don't take the *pp* marking literally; I come up at once to *mp* in order to come down again gradually. Last night I felt rather playful and did a little rubato in this passage—a hesitation after the first note of each bar—to give an added lilt so that it wouldn't sound quite square. John gave me a peculiar look; he had, after all, to play together with me. The first thing he said to me when we got off the stage was, "I'll get you for that."

One sees in these short passages how every note is worthy of technical and musical consideration. In my teaching I've never been particularly given to études and exercises. I believe that if advanced players practice the repertoire in the proper spirit, they can derive all they need in the way of technique. A Bach suite, a Brahms sonata, or the Walton

Concerto have no end of challenges. One has to be willing to isolate passages, take them apart and analyze them just as one would when working on an étude, while, of course, never forgetting the musical values.

Speaking of passages from the repertoire, what advice would you give for playing the subject of the Finale of Beethoven's Opus 59, No. 3?

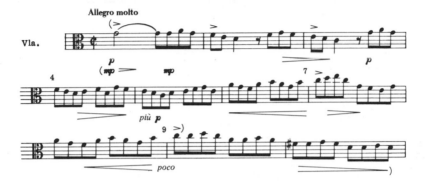

TREE I'll say something that may surprise you. My entrance is, in a way, easier than those of the other instruments. I'm free to phrase it just as I wish, and I don't have to worry about ensemble. Since they form a melodic unit, I feel that the notes that begin each of the first three bars require little accents. However, as the third bar completes the second segment of the phrase, and comes at a lower level, I play it slightly softer than the second bar. I then consciously avoid making an accent on the fourth bar; I even extend the diminuendo as far as the fifth bar so that the line can then rise in an arc—but without exaggeration—to its climax. I accentuate the high C's in bars 7 and 9, the first somewhat more than the second; I then come down just before the second violin's entrance.

Do you keep the stroke on the string?

TREE Yes; a high-bouncing spiccato would be inappropriate here. I use what I'd call an on-the-string spiccato. I play in the middle of the bow with very short strokes, pressing a little into the string; the stick jumps, but the hair hardly leaves the string. I use more bow as I go up to the climax, and then lighten the stroke almost to a real spiccato a bar before the second violin enters. However, I don't begin with the bow already on the string as I would if it were a true marcato attack. The bow only grips the string at the precise moment that I play. I want to feel that I'm giving myself an upbeat; I breathe with the bow before beginning, as though I were leading the other players.

I've heard you speak of Tartini's L'arte del arco.

TREE   Yes; it's an invaluable work, consisting of a set of variations on a theme by Corelli. I recommend it to my students. I do give a great deal of attention to the bow arm—for instance, to string crossing. When one hears an unwanted break in the line at the moment of string crossing, it's usually because the arm doesn't prepare for it in advance. The arm has a wide potential latitude of vertical movement. You can raise it to play on the left side of the string or lower it to play on the right, or you can play dead center. If the arm anticipates the string crossing by leaning in the direction of the note that's coming, a more fluid, circular motion is achieved. The difference of a quarter of an inch may be enough to put the arm in position; the wrist can then do the rest. But many players will do the exact opposite and lean the arm in the wrong direction; the result is an abrupt, angular movement.

Another bowing problem that can easily cause a disruption in the line is the tendency to make accents on separate bow strokes that have suddenly to move quickly. It's advisable to practice scales in which the time values alternate from note to note, the bow speed changing accordingly, and to take care that perfect equality of sound is maintained. This usually requires moving the bow nearer the fingerboard for the more rapid strokes. Such preparation proves invaluable when you find yourself confronted with groups of slurred notes alternating with single detached notes, as in the first movement of Brahms's G-minor Piano Quartet [Opus 25]:

One should take care here not to use too much bow on the slurred notes and to lighten the stroke immediately when playing the detached note.

The bow must again be carefully managed in the viola solo in the third movement of Brahms's B-flat-major Quartet [Opus 67]:

Every note has its own specific weight, and the bow should be free to mold the line without being held back by technical limitations. The eighths need to be dealt with lightly to avoid ungainly accents. While respecting the diminuendos within each of the first two bars, I believe there should be an overall sense of direction leading to the third bar. I thus play the second diminuendo a little more subtly than the first, to convey a feeling of connection to the third bar. Each of the three four-bar phrases traces an arc, the middle phrase [bars 5–8] reaching the highest point of intensity. This is one of the most beautiful of viola passages; the whole movement deserves detailed study to obtain just the right dynamic proportions within each phrase.

I'm sure you appreciate Brahms's good sense in indicating mutes here for all the instruments apart from the viola.

TREE   Absolutely! The only further improvement would be if the other instruments were omitted entirely.

What about Bartók's Sixth Quartet? The opening phrase is surely one of the most wonderful passages in all the quartet literature.

TREE   It is indeed. This passage is far more than just a viola solo; it's the first statement of a theme—one of the most poignant and haunting that exist. It's used as an introduction to the first three movements of the quartet and as the basis for the entire last movement. The tragic finale of this work is a crowning achievement, not only of twentieth-century music but of all music.

Would you describe in detail your approach to the opening viola passage?

TREE   The first consideration is to try to keep the bow on the string! But leaving aside the question of stage nerves, one feels a great sense of responsibility when beginning the piece—and for very good reasons. I once experimented by starting with a veiled, distant quality, as if expressing a dreamy resignation. My colleagues were, I must admit, the first to point out that this contradicted the composer's markings. "Mesto" means, simply, "sad"—it's not "misterioso"—and the *mf* clearly implies a rather forthright declaration, certainly not a pale sotto voce.

Although the *mf* governs the initial tone color, as there is no other dynamic marking for five bars, it's important to find room within the *mf* range for shaping and nuance. The opening phrase develops in intensity to the middle of the second bar and then gradually subsides to the fourth bar; so we have a rainbow at the very outset. At the fourth bar I would begin more quietly and little by little give a feeling of crescendo, at first with the left hand and finally—in bar 6, where Bartók gives his sanction—with the bow.

Do you make a gradual diminuendo from the forte in bar 8 to the end of the phrase?

TREE   That's an interesting question. Bartók clearly marks *f–mf–p,* and I'm inclined to think that even though the line descends, one shouldn't do the normal thing and make a gradual diminuendo. I try to come down in terraces: subito *mf,* then subito *p.* Having arrived at the piano, I do, however, allow a very little crescendo to lead into the accented

A flat in bar 12. This is so subtle a matter that I'm hesitant even to mark it; it's only that one should feel that the A flat doesn't come out of nowhere. The last note—even though it's *pp*, legato, and at the very tail end of the phrase—requires a little articulation, a slight touch of the bow. Otherwise it risks not being heard.

This subtle sense of give and take applies not only to the dynamics but to the rhythm as well. The fact that the metronome marking refers to eighth notes doesn't mean that every eighth beat moves rigidly; one wants to keep a natural, flowing line.

The long legato slurs convey Bartók's expressive intent, but they're not very practical from the standpoint of bowing. The instrument won't sing readily unless the bow is changed more often. However, the changes should be made as discreetly as possible so as not to disrupt the legato line. The bow change I've indicated in bar 3 doesn't look very nice on paper. Since those three notes are the end of the phrase, you would expect them to be slurred together; great care has to be taken to avoid an accent in the middle of the bar. A whole bow is needed in bar 7 for the crescendo on the long note. When arriving at the forte [bar 8], if I feel a need for more bow, I may change more frequently (as indicated under the staff). During the last four bars the line becomes quieter, the texture more floating, and I therefore leave the slurs intact, as in the score.

In some places my fingering is a little unorthodox. In bar 10 a 1–2 extension enables me to stay in second position and reach across the string for the G flat without having to shift. In bar 11 I contract the hand to play 4–1; this allows me to play the accented A flat with the third finger rather than the fourth and hence to be more sure of the quality of sound. These are small examples of creeping around the fingerboard à la Zimbalist.

Violists owe a debt of gratitude to Bartók—and to Hindemith, Vaughan Williams, Tippett, Walton, Bloch, and other twentieth-century composers who have contributed so much to our repertoire. But above all we must be thankful to Mozart. Seen in historical perspective, one could almost say that he liberated the viola. He was years ahead of his time in his writing for the instrument. Nowadays we tend to take for granted the existence of his Sinfonia Concertante for Violin and Viola, but it's simply an astonishing work from every standpoint.

Do you play the viola part in the Sinfonia Concertante with the original scordatura, tuning the instrument up a semitone?

TREE   No, I don't. Mozart's intention was to allow the viola to use more open strings and therefore take on greater brilliance. With today's improved standard in viola technique the scordatura is no longer a necessity. But I have a personal reason as well for not retuning the instrument. Call it what you will, a gift or a curse: I have what is commonly known as perfect pitch. I find it disconcerting to read the piece in the key of D while hearing it in E flat. If I were a singer and had to learn a complicated twelve-tone work in a hurry, I imagine my perfect pitch could be an asset. But when it comes to transposition, perfect pitch is a decided liability. A good sense of relative pitch is all that a musician needs, and it spares one the curse of associating every printed note with a fixed sound.

Mozart also treated the viola as a full-fledged concertante instrument in the Trio for Clarinet, Viola, and Piano [K. 498] and the Divertimento for String Trio [K. 563]—both masterpieces. He expanded the role of the viola in his later quartets. Above all, he left us his viola quintets. Beethoven, Mendelssohn, Brahms, and Dvořák all followed suit. Taken as a whole, Mozart's quintets may be his greatest chamber music for strings. However, I must say that whenever I play a Mozart quartet I'm convinced at the moment that it's the best work he's ever written. Nevertheless, the quintets are perhaps more unusual, in the sense that the added viola contributes a great deal in terms of texture. If there's such a place as a viola players' Hall of Fame, we would have to elect Mozart as its guardian angel.

From all you've said, I can hazard a guess that you don't regret your decision to have switched over to the viola.

TREE   Just try to pry it away from me.

You mentioned before that the viola may even have brought out another side of your nature. What sort of effect do you think playing the viola in the quartet has had upon you personally?

TREE   I don't want to sound like a pop psychologist or delve into matters that are beyond me, but being a pivotal or middle-voiced member of a quartet provides a special vantage point from which it's possible to view more than one side of an issue in clear perspective. Whether or not this has affected my personality I cannot say. But it's a joy to be part of the process of shaping and being shaped. We're touching here on the real dynamics of quartet playing.

John Dalley

What are some of the common misconceptions about the role of the second violin in a quartet?

DALLEY First and foremost, that the player taking on this position does so because he or she is not quite up to playing first violin. In the old days, it's true, a quartet was often made up of a soloist and three other players, the least of whom was usually the second violinist. Most present-day quartets do, however, consist of four equally gifted players. Nonetheless, the idea that the second violin plays a subordinate role is not entirely laid to rest. In fact, people still come up to me after concerts who think that a "second violin" is a different kind of instrument from a "first violin."

What advice would you give a young player entering a quartet as second violinist?

DALLEY Not to assume the psychological makeup of a so-called second fiddle. William Primrose had a good idea when he proposed that the term "second violin" be changed to "the other violin"; the whole hierarchical misconception should be done away with. It's best when both violinists in a quartet are equally matched and the second violinist has, in fact, something of a plucky, aggressive approach. As Primrose wrote, "The procedure is *not* to sit down on the chair and be modest."

In fact, a critic once referred to you as a "dangerously good" second violinist.

DALLEY Bless his heart!

The second violinist in a quartet must be prepared to do a good deal of leading. In the Budapest Quartet, for instance, the first violinist Joseph Roisman wanted as much as possible to be left free of that sort of thing; it therefore fell to the second violinist, Alexander Schneider, to take over much of the responsibility for leading. It's rather uncomfortable for cellists to lead; they're more rooted physically in one position. The second violinist becomes the logical choice, particularly for rhythmic figures that primarily concern the lower voices.

I often have to read Arnold's mind to make sure that we'll all be together. The biggest problem in playing an accompaniment lies not in finding the dynamic balance, which is relatively easy to adjust, but in establishing the right rhythmic relationship with the solo voice. The melodic line will often be written in longer note-values than the accompanying figures, which may, especially in the classical literature, consist of repeated eighth or sixteenth notes. Obviously, the tempo of the solo voice is subject to whatever you establish for it; that's a tricky business, because you have to anticipate your colleague's wishes. Take, for instance, the Allegro theme from the first movement of Mozart's C-major Quartet, K. 465 [see page 56]. I give the lead to assure the ensemble of eighth notes between the second violin and the viola. But Michael and I have to keep our ears open; should Arnold play his melody slightly faster or slower, we will adjust right away. We treat the cello solo at the beginning of Beethoven's Opus 59, No. 1 similarly [see page 57]. An accompaniment must always be in absolute sympathy with the theme as it's being played at the given moment. For example, at the beginning of Schubert's A-minor Quartet—

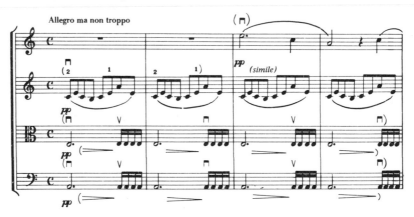

—the three lower voices establish the tempo and character of the piece two bars before the first violin even enters, yet we have to correspond to his conception.

How do you interpret this most beautiful of accompaniment figures?

DALLEY   I think of the phrasing as five notes plus three. I do, however, follow the bowing as the printed slur indicates, and the inner phrasing is more a matter of thought than of execution. A particularly good fingering is to alternate between second and first position, not actually shifting but letting the hand move in a supple way between the two. The

first five notes are thus played on the G string, the last three on the D
string, and this provides just the right phrasing. The real rhythmic impetus comes mainly from the viola and the cello. They articulate their
sixteenths on the string, as if tapping a muted drum, always making a
diminuendo on the dotted half note. I have to fit in with this hushed
atmosphere and look for a very ethereal sound. I try to imagine that this
music was there to begin with, that I'm not actually beginning it. It's
something like existence. Existence is there; you don't start it.

When a full-fledged melodic line finally does come the second violinist's way, it's often in the middle or low register, where, alas, it's difficult to be heard. Take the following passage from the first movement
of Beethoven's Opus 127:

At bar 171 the theme, begun four bars earlier by the first violin, is taken
over by the second violin, playing two octaves lower. One has to cut
through a thick texture that includes a first-violin obbligato; the double-
stops tend to obscure the melody even further. The second violin has
to treat the piano here as an expressive mezzo forte, and everyone else
should scale way down.

The player is further disadvantaged in such passages by having, so
to speak, to quickly fill the breach when seizing upon the melodic line.
The second violinist's position is like that of the third horn in *Till Eulen-
spiegel*. The first horn has three chances to play the *Till* theme, the third

horn only one. He has to play it just as well, but he gets only one shot.

A special sort of problem arises when both violins play figures of more or less equal melodic importance. For example, in the slow movement of Beethoven's Opus 59, No. 2 there's a wonderful counterpoint between the two violins:

My notes rise above those of the first violin, and I don't want to cover him. On the other hand, my part is also melodic. The nature of the writing helps us here. The main melody in the first violin is very sustained, while my figure rises and falls in waves. This allows me to vary my dynamic level and make more ups and downs than Arnold does. I may, for instance, make an expressive accent on the half-note B and a crescendo to the half-note D in the following bar. These nuances bring my part into relief without my having to play too loudly in general.

The fourth variation in Schubert's "Death and the Maiden" poses a similar question. Which is of greater importance: the slightly altered theme in the second violin or the beautiful first-violin obbligato? Both should be heard, but to what degree? I want my presence to be felt, without overly intruding on the first violin. Once again, I do this by letting my nuances rise and fall with the curves of the phrase:

The whole variation—there are bird calls in the second part—is filled with variety, loveliness, and charm.

The ability to project is, of course, dependent in part on the instrument itself. Your violin has an unusual warmth and power of projection in the middle and low registers. Would you tell me something about it?

DALLEY   My fiddle was made by Nicolas Lupot in Paris in 1810. It has a richness of timbre that one might associate with an Italian instrument; but unlike some Italian violins, even great ones, it doesn't give way under a lot of pressure. It's hardy and robust and has a lot of resistance. One needs an instrument that can match the outgoing quality of the other instruments in the quartet. The second violinist's role is chameleonlike: when playing on the lower strings he has to be able to blend with the dark sonority of the viola. In fact, when in the lower register, I often have to think like a violist in order to cut through; one develops that as a way of survival. One must then be able to change one's color in an instant to match the timbre of the first violin.

A sensitive first violinist can help by going out of his way, where appropriate, to blend with the second violin, rather than always expecting the second violin to blend with him. At such times it's a question not only of the first violin reducing volume but of his finding a quieter color—playing on a less brilliant string or toning down the intensity of vibrato. A lot of the success of the second violin depends on the first violin. We're fortunate in our quartet that Arnold understands such things so well. Perhaps that explains why I'm thought of as a "dangerously good" second violinist.

The second violinist's pivotal role concerns not only rhythm and sonority but bowing as well. You have to be ready to adjust to your colleagues' phrasing; and if this entails unexpected bowing changes, you have to change bows accordingly and carry on even if you find yourself in the wrong part of the bow—say, at the frog when making a diminuendo to pianissimo.

Do you often find yourself in that kind of predicament?

DALLEY   All the time! But, frankly, I rather like it, because it keeps you thinking and aware of what's going on. Perhaps the ideal would be to achieve a consistently high level of inspiration with bowings that never deviate. But there's also something to be said for keeping things fresh and alive and taking chances.

You've also spoken about the value of being flexible when it comes to fingerings.

DALLEY   One sometimes has to be! I was once put to the test when, during a concert in which I was playing first violin, I experienced such pain in my fourth finger that I couldn't even let it touch the string. It was later diagnosed as tendinitis and, with medication, was healed in four or five days. In any case, on the spur of the moment I had to change all the fingerings, playing the whole program with only three fingers. I assumed that my difficulties must have been obvious. But when we came offstage after the last piece and I asked Michael whether he had noticed anything unusual about my playing, he replied, "Not at all," and assured me that he had found nothing amiss. I'm not quite sure that that speaks well for my playing in general.

In fact, everyone is so much in awe of your resourcefulness on that occasion that they hope you'll try it again, but next time using only two fingers.

DALLEY   Don't get nasty, David.

Many a dedicated amateur chamber-music player has a dread of rhythmic complexities, syncopations being the main bugbear. Have you any advice, for instance, on the syncopated variation in the Finale of Mozart's D-minor Quartet [K. 421]?

DALLEY I would concentrate on the eighth-note pulsation maintained by the viola and first violin to make sure that my rhythm is very strict. I would also direct the sixteenth notes forward—not faster but with a sense of crescendo. When actually playing the figure, I don't think of it as being in a duple rhythm, though it comes out sounding that way.

When rhythmic complexities arise in a quartet, it doesn't necessarily help to rehearse slowly; that just gives you the same complexity in a slower tempo, and if you have counter-rhythms this can even increase the difficulty. In such cases it's best to play the passage up to tempo but only in short segments. It's also sometimes helpful to think of a metric pattern differently from how it appears on the printed page. In the Prestissimo, con sordino from Bartók's Fourth Quartet, the second violin, playing double-stops, is suddenly given a counter-rhythm to the regular $\frac{6}{8}$ pulsation [bars 181–183]:

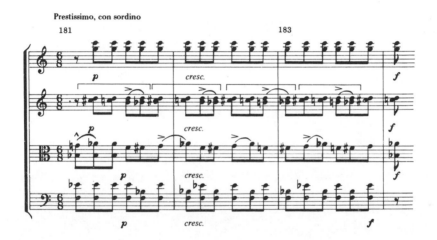

I find that this passage becomes much easier to execute if you rebar it in your own mind. I imagine four groups in $\frac{4}{8}$ time [as indicated by brackets] with one eighth note left over at the end of bar 183. If you come out wrong, you're sunk, but it's worth the risk.

The Alla bulgarese movement from Bartók's Fifth Quartet has a peculiar time signature and rather difficult offbeat figures:

I find that the 4 + 2 + 3 pattern inhibits me from piecing it all together, so I just ignore that indication and think of it as being in a regular ⅜ time (3 + 3 + 3) and accentuate the fourth eighth note, as I've indicated in the rewritten bar. It comes out sounding as the composer intended it, and it's much easier to play. I think we'd save a lot of rehearsal time if we all thought of it in this way, but my colleagues aren't unanimous on the point.

How would you describe your philosophy as a teacher?

DALLEY   I like to give a student as much liberty as possible and adapt the course of studies to his or her specific needs. Some teachers believe in putting all students through a prescribed regimen of études and exercises; even if some of the material is redundant, all possible problem areas will be covered. I personally think that it saves time to focus on the student's actual problems and to choose the études accordingly. One can derive most technical skills through the repertoire itself. The vast violin literature is an enormous plus—consider only Paganini and Bach! I also encourage my students to work out their own fingerings and bowings. An essential part of the learning process lies in developing the ability to think for oneself.

I would say that, in general, perhaps the greatest enemy of good string playing is tension. Tension can strike in many places. One often finds it in the vibrato; there may be a tightening in the arm, the wrist, or, very often, the thumb. The bow arm can suffer too. Some players think that if they just change the way they hold the bow, their problems will automatically disappear. But sometimes what's needed is only a little release of tension: perhaps in the shoulder, the elbow, the wrist, or in the fingers themselves. In many cases a psychological aspect also has to be taken into account.

It's important that any signs of undue tension be caught at the beginning. I myself was fortunate in having good teachers right from the start.

At what age did you begin?

DALLEY   At three and a half. Both my parents took a keen interest in my musical education. My father, Orien Dalley, was on the music faculty of the University of Wisconsin and later became the conductor of the Wichita Symphony, and my mother was a professional cellist and teacher. The man who had the strongest influence on my development was my first teacher, Virgil Person. Interestingly enough, he had never before taught a young child. My subsequent teachers were equally fine: David Robertson, who went on to become the director of the Oberlin Conservatory, and Otokar Cádek, a superb violinist of Czech background whom I first met at the National Music Camp in Interlochen, Michigan. Cádek taught at the University of Alabama, and my family accepted his invitation that I live in his home in Tuscaloosa. I studied with him while attending my last three years of high school as a part-time student.

Did you begin playing chamber music at an early age?

DALLEY   While still in junior high I had a weekly quartet session with friends who played in a youth orchestra my father conducted. We covered the whole basic classical repertoire. For young string players who want to increase their musical awareness and sensitivity, playing quartets is an invaluable experience. I also gained a good deal during six summers at Interlochen—not only in regard to sight-reading and orchestral playing but in social values, which one wouldn't get while studying alone. It was useful, too, to be able to see my own rate of development in relation to that of my peers.

I subsequently spent six years at Curtis, studying—as Michael did—with Efrem Zimbalist. Just being in contact with a man of such charisma had a most positive effect. I had heard horror stories that he was extremely severe and sarcastic, but, fortunately, I never saw any evidence of that. It's true that when he didn't like something he would keep at it until he was satisfied; but he was always an absolute gentleman with me. During the lessons, while watching your bowings and fingerings, he would sit at the piano and play from memory the accompaniments to all the concertos. It was a little spooky to be in the presence of a man who could concentrate on all those things at once. So naturally you had tremendous respect for him. He had a liberal approach to teaching and always accepted a student's effort if he found it valid in its own right. Some teachers use a fixed set of fingerings for a given work, and they pass this on to all their students. Zimbalist often used the score the student himself brought and sometimes found fault with his own edition, saying, "This fingering isn't very good; let's look for something better." Typical of his broad-mindedness he never asked me to change my bow grip, although it was different from his. He respected the fact that it worked for me.

Would you describe the way in which you hold the bow?

DALLEY   If you want to put a tag on it, I'd say it's close to the Franco-Belgian school; the bow touches between the first and second knuckles of the index finger. I find that although the more slanted bow-hold of the Russian school facilitates playing at the tip, it brings the wrist too high for playing comfortably at the frog. In fact, Zimbalist would ask me, "How do you manage so well at the frog?" And I would reply, "I don't know, but how do you play so marvelously at the tip?"

A good way to develop one's bow control is to take a basic stroke and purposefully make it difficult—to try to execute it in various lengths in different parts of the bow. Even if a stroke feels awkward at first, it helps to hone one's skills. It's rare for young players to explore all of these possibilities, caught up as they are in the routine of lessons, études, and learning concertos. But if you keep on making such demands on yourself—just as singers constantly try to extend their range and develop their flexibility—you'll widen your repertoire of bowing and gain greater freedom as an interpreter.

You could, for example, take a standard spiccato stroke and do it too far towards the tip, trying to preserve the same buoyancy; or you could take it to the frog. Most players don't want to execute any of the so-called back-and-forth strokes at the frog. But when I try to help students improve their changes of bow I ask them to do it at the extreme frog, right under the hand rather than in the middle of the bow, where it feels comfortable.

I also give a lot of attention to the articulation of the left hand and urge my students to apply left-hand pizzicato to the violin just as Casals did to the cello. On the piano every note that's struck has equal clarity. But on a stringed instrument there's an inequality between ascending and descending passages. When a passage ascends, the finger strikes the string, creating a natural articulation. But when a passage descends, the sound is often produced by lifting the finger, so there is no resultant articulation. To compensate for this, it's useful in descending passages to lift the finger with a slight pizzicato action. It's a subtle thing and shouldn't be exaggerated; the finger just brushes the string as it comes off. But it helps greatly in the projection of sound, particularly for articulating quick notes in legato passages.

Another important aspect of articulation is the enunciation of the first note of a phrase. As Casals insisted, "The first note must always be heard." When the first note is quick or comes on an offbeat it needs special attention. In a passage such as the following, from the Scherzo of Beethoven's Opus 127—

—while the main point of rhythmic emphasis (ᴜ) falls on the bar line, the first sixteenth note needs clear articulation (>). My accent is meant not to distort the natural lilt of the phrase but to compensate for acoustical loss. Similarly, when I play the fugal subject in the Finale of Beethoven's Opus 59, No. 3, I take care to enunciate the first eighth in each figure. This is particularly important because mine is the second entrance, and I must contend with the countersubject in the viola:

On paper the accents appear to contradict the natural phrasing, but in performance they sound just right.

I believe that it's indispensable for every musician's studies to include a good course in harmony. Single-line players in particular tend to think in linear terms and are sometimes not sufficiently sensitive to the harmonic motion around them. Harmony and counterpoint were taught at Curtis in such a way as to develop the ear as fully as possible. The emphasis was always on working away from the piano. I find it amazing that Delius, when blind and paralyzed, could continue composing as he did, dictating whole compositions to his amanuensis, Eric Fenby. He specified every chord, from the lowest note to the highest, and yet each chord maintained a fine sense of melodic voice-leading.

The second violinist often has to think in both dimensions, the vertical and the linear. It helps to have a cellist in the quartet who provides a strong bass, because the chords are felt from the bottom up. That's the outgrowth of the figured bass, where the bass instigated what happened harmonically—and the quartet is constructed similarly. One of the most illuminating things any musician can do is to study Bach's chorales. When you take the theme and bass and remove the other voices you have a puzzle: what harmonies should be put in? Then you go to Bach's solution, and it's often astounding. He never ceases to surprise you.

One of my most valuable learning experiences came when, at the age of twenty-two, I began a four-year teaching stint at the Oberlin Conservatory while playing in the Oberlin Quartet. When twenty kids come to you with all sorts of instrumental problems, it keeps you on your toes trying to stay ahead of them. This helped me to clarify my own thoughts about violin playing. My experience teaching at Oberlin was probably more instructive for me than for my students.

What do you find to be the chief difficulties confronting inexperienced quartet players?

DALLEY   One often has to help them approach music from a new vantage point. After all, during the early years of development, you try to build on what God has given you in the way of instrumental talent. You work on your technique; you're probably force-fed many things, and you may play a lot by rote. You're handed the Mendelssohn Concerto with all the fingerings and bowings worked out for you, and you learn the piece accordingly. But when you play in a group for the first time and have to analyze a work, it's something entirely different; you have to start processing into sound what's on the page, and understanding not only your own part but all four parts. Young people are often bamboozled by this—it's such a new experience for them. So I tell students to take up the score and try to understand it, try to envision the kind of sound that's wanted at each moment. That's the first step.

If your imagination is always active and you have certain expectations of sounds in your ear, you will be able to develop a wide palette of colors: the variety in nuance, sonority, bowing, and vibrato that the music needs. It's rather like the "method" school of acting; you have to think yourself into the role, enter into the composer's mind. You can't just think about tomorrow's grocery list.

Arnold Steinhardt

Perhaps we could begin by discussing your teachers and the ways you feel they've influenced you.

STEINHARDT I've had five violin teachers, and each has been important to me in his own way. The first three lived in Los Angeles, where I was born and raised. I began with Carl Moldrem, a well-known teacher of young children, who had delightful and original ways of communicating with beginners. From the age of nine to fourteen I worked with Peter Meremblum, a Russian violinist who had at one time been a student of Leopold Auer. Meremblum, who had a rather tempestuous personality, led me through the violin repertoire, often in dramatic ways. At one unforgettable lesson I excused some poor intonation on the grounds that my violin was out of tune; he simply mistuned my instrument even further and then played perfectly in tune on it. Meremblum also conducted a youth orchestra, which, through his musicianship and personality, became an enormous musical influence in the area. The list of artists he cajoled into appearing with this group of youngsters reads like a *Who's Who* of music: Heifetz, Rubinstein, Piatigorsky. . . . Much of the great Russian orchestral music was included in our programs, and these works left a deep impression on me.

My next teacher was Toscha Seidel, a once-famous virtuoso who as a child prodigy had been compared to Heifetz. His temperamental nature tended to strike fear into a student's heart, but the great strength of his teaching lay in the playing itself. Losing patience with me, he would often play through entire pieces with a warmth and abandon I shall never forget.

At seventeen I continued my studies at the Curtis Institute with Ivan Galamian, an extraordinary pedagogue. Owing to the fact that he had a great number of students, the lessons were businesslike and lasted exactly one hour—no more, no less; but there was a focus and discipline that made them seem much longer. Galamian put much emphasis on the projection of sound. He wanted you mentally to break down the walls of the practice studio and learn how to enunciate the music in such a way that it would project to the last row of a large auditorium. He was insistent that the beginnings of notes be given real definition. The violin string, lying there passively, is reluctant to move. In physics one would say that a body at rest tends to stay at rest. When one wants instantaneous, clear articulation, the string has to be grabbed almost as if the bow had teeth or claws. Galamian always stressed the importance of utilizing the fingers of the bow hand. He asked that even very fast detached notes be practiced in slow motion: the bow was to be set firmly on the string, while the hair was pushed back and forth by the fingers to assure the tactile sense of really getting "into the string" and gripping it. Then, with the release of the bow, the string would spring into vibration, giving the note a crisp beginning. The softer the passage, the more the bow stroke becomes the responsibility of the fingers rather than the arm. In fact, when he saw I wasn't using my fingers or wrist, he would feign a limp and hobble across the floor, using the hip and knee joints but not the ankle joint or toes—and, of course, it looked ridiculous. It was a simple but dramatic way of demonstrating that suppleness is essential to good playing.

Galamian gave a lot of attention to the basic concerto and virtuoso repertoires; he knew that young musicians must learn quickly, that it becomes increasingly difficult to learn these concertos when you're past twenty-five. Some people speak of a certain doctrinaire aspect to Galamian's teaching. It's true that when you studied a concerto he would usually say, "Go to my assistant and copy out the fingerings." But he knew that when we left him we weren't going to adhere rigidly to all the fingerings. And I must say that his students weren't all given the same material to work on at the same level of development; he would select specific studies according to individual needs. If he was more interested in teaching violin technique than musical interpretation, at least this left you free to interpret as you wished. Although he always systematically taught the same basic principles of technique, his students didn't become carbon copies stamped out of a Galamian machine. Perlman, Zukerman, and any number of his students have developed their own musical personalities and individual sounds.

I note that your way of holding the bow differs from Galamian's.

STEINHARDT   Yes, my bow grip has changed considerably since my Galamian days. He liked the fingers to be spread, with the first finger somewhat separated from the others. He rightly felt that this gave a wonderful purchase on the string. But I found that this position put a certain strain on my hand; my wrist tended to tighten. I eventually changed to a less spread position, and this helped my bow hand to become more relaxed and supple. Like John, I let the index finger rest on the bow between the first and second knuckles. There are, however, Galamian students who still use his bow grip after twenty or thirty years' playing and are very happy with it. As in everything, you find your own way.

Soon after leaving Curtis I won the Leventritt Competition and was heard by George Szell, who invited me to become assistant concertmaster of the Cleveland Orchestra, next to Josef Gingold. My Cleveland years—1959 to '64—were an invaluable learning experience. Szell was a great trainer of orchestras; he was fanatic about achieving perfect orchestral balance. Under his direction one realized that an orchestra is actually playing chamber music. In fact, as I see it, there are elements of chamber music in *all* music, solo playing as well. Take the slow movement of the Bartók Concerto, where the first variation of the theme involves the violin in a dialogue with the timpani; or the Finale of the Beethoven Concerto, where the violin plays an accompaniment to the bassoon. In fact, there are many passages throughout the Beethoven Concerto where the violin has accompaniment figures. Even when playing unaccompanied music—whether Bach, Reger, Ysaÿe, or Bartók— one must constantly differentiate and clarify the voices. That's chamber music in the truest sense.

Although Szell was reticent in his personal relationship with members of the orchestra, he took an interest in my artistic development. I had the privilege of performing concertos by Beethoven and Mozart with him, the work sessions being as unforgettable as the concerts themselves. Seeing that I didn't play some of the slurs and grace notes of the Mozart A-major Concerto in accordance with the score, he suggested that I go to the source at the Library of Congress in Washington. Holding Mozart's autograph in my hands, I was able to see note by note how far editions can wander from the composer's intentions. Szell's scholarship and attention to detail were hallmarks of his musical personality.

While in Cleveland I worked and performed with the pianist Arthur Loesser, a superb musician who brought an uncommonly thorough approach to interpretation. He would comment on my violin playing from a pianist's point of view, giving particular stress to elements of harmony and counterpoint. Once, when I had played Bach's D-minor Partita for him, he asked, "Do you know how to dance these movements?" Of course I didn't. So he got up from his chair and said, "Let's start with the Allemande," and proceeded to dance each movement for me. With his help I began to see that there's a sense of dance, strong or subtle, in all music—an element of pulse, of lilt, of direction, of movement.

On Szell's recommendation I studied for a summer with Joseph Szigeti, who was then living in Clarens, Switzerland. Szigeti was a truly great artist, and I would urge musicians of the new generation to acquaint themselves with his recordings, among them the Mozart D-major, the Mendelssohn, the Brahms, and the Prokofiev concertos.

I heard Szigeti play only once. It was near the end of his career, and during the first part of the concert—though his extraordinary musicianship was always apparent—some nerves were evident. But after the intermission he returned to play Bach's D-minor Partita with a sovereign command. The Chaconne had a towering majesty that I've never heard equalled.

STEINHARDT   No artist could play with a more stirring sense of vision. I had expected that in his teaching he would focus on lofty matters of interpretation. I was, however, surprised by the amount of attention he gave to problems of fingering and bowing, for which he devised fascinating solutions. He would go to great lengths to differentiate colors; he spoke of "étages"—steps or levels—and would say, "This phrase is for soprano; keep it on one string. The next is for alto; play it on another string." He also stressed the fact that the violin doesn't only sing; it speaks. He taught the art of parlando with the bow. A favorite game of his was to invent words that matched the rhythmic configuration of a phrase, drawing attention to natural points of emphasis. This principle can be applied to music of all periods.

To Mozart, for instance, whose instrumental music was strongly influenced by Italian vocal art and speech rhythms.

STEINHARDT   Absolutely! That consideration is often neglected in playing Mozart.

The musical experience that perhaps influenced me the most was Marlboro, which is also to say Rudolf Serkin—the interpreter, the personality. Serkin's approach to music, like Szell's, complemented the influence of my early teachers of the play-from-the-heart Russian school. As a German-trained musician, Serkin had a deep commitment to form and structure as well as to feeling; color was never used for color's sake alone. It's marvelous to witness Serkin in action: the depth of his study, the seriousness of his rehearsals, the intensity of his performances. In big works such as the "Hammerklavier" Sonata it's as if a tornado sweeps across the stage. There was much to be learned from the idea that profound scholarship can be combined with fervent communication in performance. This is the case with Serkin, as it was with Casals, whose visits to Marlboro coincided with the years I was there. With both artists one found warmth and power of imagination allied to a pure and dedicated spirit, the personality being utterly at one with the music. Marlboro also provided invaluable contact with such musicians as Marcel Moyse and Felix Galimir—not only powerful musical forces in their own right but also direct links to us from their own past, which included personal contact with figures such as Debussy, Ravel, Schoenberg, Berg, and Webern. All of us in the quartet owe much to Marlboro—to the artistic camaraderie, the indelible impressions, the encouragement we found there.

What suggestions would you offer to someone undertaking the role of first violin in a quartet?

STEINHARDT   Above all, I'd say that there's not just one role. Like actors, musicians have to play many roles at different times. It's dangerous to think of yourself as the "first violin." One moment you may be a soloist; the next, an accompanist. There are, for example, many occasions when the leading voice will pass from the first violin in the upper register to another instrument in a lower register, the first violin meanwhile continuing on the E string with a secondary voice. I often notice that in inexperienced groups the first violinist will play only a little softer at that moment, but not softly enough to dispel the impression that the first violin still has the dominant voice. A much greater effort is needed to rebalance. In chamber music you have to apply two sets of dynamics: one for solo passages, one for accompaniment passages. Even if you're playing in piano as a soloist, the moment your part suddenly becomes an accompaniment, that piano should drop down dramatically. Take the following passage from the Finale of Beethoven's Opus 132:

According to the printed dynamics it would seem that the first violin should rise in a crescendo to the forte [upbeat to bar 64] and assert itself there. In fact, when the forte comes, the lower voices are of far greater importance than the reiterated high E's; yet the first violin will be more prominent owing to the brilliance of the register. I therefore come down to piano at that moment, not forgetting to make a diminuendo on each syncopation. Then, on the D sharp [upbeat to bar 68], where piano is marked, I actually regain more tone as I take over the leading voice. Throughout the coda I have to be careful not to overpower the cello, even when I join it in octaves to play the melody.

One of the difficulties in forming a string quartet is that many violinists who've reached a certain level of attainment don't want to play the second violin. Yet the second violinist must be just as gifted and have all the same skills. It needs a certain kind of personality to take on the role of second violin—someone with no less of an ego but a different kind of ego, who appreciates the inner workings of a clock as well as its exterior. I've always thought that the easiest person to replace in a string quartet is the first violinist. When John, Michael, and I got together, we didn't know who was going to play first, second, or viola; and, in fact, any one of us could have done any of those things.

I understand that your Storioni violin has had a long quartet history.

STEINHARDT   Yes. It was in the Budapest Quartet for many years and was played both by the Budapest's original first violinist, Emil Hauser, and by his successor, Joseph Roisman. So whenever I take up the instrument to practice, it tells me, "Why bother? I know the entire quartet literature by heart!" The Storioni is the fifth violin I've played on during our quartet's existence. This relates to what we spoke of earlier: the need for an instrument used in quartet playing to have solo qualities. My previous violins were a Pressenda, a Seraphin, a Guadagnini, and a Guarnerius "del Gesù." Each time I graduated upwards in quality and robustness. Like many young professionals, I made the mistake of being seduced by the beauty of sound directly under my ear and was offended by any kind of stridency or roughness; I failed to realize that most of that falls away when the instrument is heard by an audience in a hall. A good instrument will have both quality of sound and strength of character. My Storioni isn't really a violin but a viola that's been cut down. Its shape is unusual but very beautiful. The sound is powerful and dark. It's particularly rich in overtones and sometimes almost roars at you.

What are some of the principles you stress in your teaching?

STEINHARDT   I'm concerned with basics; I want my students to play in tune. No more important service can be rendered to the composer and to the work. It's hard to do; I put this as one of the first priorities. Then I work with the student to find his or her most natural physical approach to the instrument. The violin is an awkward instrument to hold and to play; poor habits can easily develop, causing strain in both the right and the left arm. So I stress "athletic" ability in the sense of doing things easily and letting the gestures be as direct and efficient as possible. I believe that if you called in a golf or tennis coach who had a fine sense of basic body motions, he would be able to tell you what you're doing wrong as a violinist, where you are making extraneous effort. I ask my students to stand in front of a mirror—not to look at their gorgeous faces but to study their playing carefully, to distinguish between what is awkward and what is natural.

Would you change a player's physical position that seems to function well even if it is different from your own?

STEINHARDT   Most people will not play as I do in all respects because I'm six feet, three inches tall and have large hands. Some of my students are delicate young girls, five feet, two inches tall, with small hands.

Do you attract that type?

STEINHARDT   I don't know . . . I won't comment on that. But every-body has a different hand. A fingering that works for me won't always be suitable for someone else.

   Once these fundamentals are attended to, I of course try to give my students a well-grounded musical approach and help them to under-stand the possibilities of phrasing. Finally, I encourage them to trust their individuality, and try to set them on the path to being themselves.

This last point—also stressed by your colleagues in the quartet—is something very few teachers give attention to.

STEINHARDT   Well, it *is* hard to do. My wife once told me after hearing me teach, "You know, you're a little dictator, always saying, 'Do this, do that.' I wanted to defend those poor students." "But they're in doubt about their playing," I protested; "I really *have* to tell them what to do." After all, you spend much of your life developing your particular way of playing, and then, even if you don't admit it to yourself, some part of you is saying, "There's no other way to do it." Coupled with this is the fact that the student is probably studying with you because he admires your way of playing. Perhaps it's only natural that students should pass through an imitative stage. But by the time they're advanced and about to become professional, you really have to open their eyes to what is unique in them. You should be able to see what a student is, to recognize that a student is something that you are not—possibly even something that you don't want to be—but to understand and appreciate his or her innate way of doing things and to encourage that process. In short, to let them go their own way.

You mentioned helping your students to understand the possibilities of phrasing. Would you comment more fully on that?

STEINHARDT   It's of course a matter of prime importance. Players who greatly influenced me in this respect were Casals, Szigeti, and Schnabel. I would listen with fascination to some of the slow movements from Schnabel's recordings of Beethoven sonatas—for instance, the Largo e mesto from Opus 10, No. 3; the way he manipulates the phrases and voices is extraordinary. It's said that when practicing, Schnabel would sometimes spend hours on two or three bars; it was like putting small amounts of powder on a scale to get the exact measurements. Listening to these performances sets one thinking.

What general principles would you adopt in reference to building a phrase?

STEINHARDT   A phrase should be a complete, coherent thought; it should have a beginning, a middle, and an end. No part of it should just go on mindlessly. You should be conscious of the role of every note and sense its relation to other notes in the phrase; there's always a cause and effect. You have to be an architect and a workman at the same time; you mustn't put a brick in the middle of the building without thinking about all that came before and must come afterwards. If you're an architect-builder and your building collapses, you may be sued and sent to jail. In music there's no less of a sense of responsibility.

Musicians often talk about finding the "long line" of a piece. I believe, however, that the first priority is to understand how to shape a melody. And melody is made up of moment-to-moment contours—contours which must have their proper proportions. Once you've achieved that, you can concern yourself with the overall line. Marcel

Moyse—not only a great flutist but a great teacher—used to give wood-wind classes at Marlboro that proved positively illuminating. He would take a melody that might last fifteen seconds and devote an hour to examining it in detail. He would discuss every note in relation to the proportions of the phrase, show the degree of tension residing in every interval. It was particularly interesting for me as a string player to attend such classes. String players often get caught up in stylistic considerations pertaining to the instrument—a certain kind of tone, of vibrato, of glis-sando—all of which runs the risk of taking us away from the music itself.

Some musicians fear that a detailed examination of a phrase may smother spontaneity and lead to self-consciousness. That certainly wasn't the case with Moyse, Serkin, or Casals. Maybe it really works the other way round. Perhaps spontaneity depends upon a real percep-tion of the musical line and its possibilities. The idea that it's enough just to rely on inspiration is a trap when it comes to interpreting music. When the composer wrote a work, he felt the function of every note. The interpreter has to enter as much as possible into the composer's creative workshop.

In shaping a phrase one has to consider three factors: the melodic, the harmonic, and the rhythmic. I personally find it helpful to envisage a melody in the form of a line drawing. The rise and fall of the notes often—though not always—imply a subtle rise and fall of dynamic in-tensity. But these ups and downs mustn't sound predictable; the musical drawing should have aesthetic interest, imagination as well as order. If the hills and valleys repeat themselves in exactly the same way, you get something that's rather boring. So we come to the principle of variety in the shaping process. For example, if a note reappears during the course of a phrase, it may well be fulfilling a different function and should perhaps be played at a different level of intensity. I find that it helps to sing a melody out loud. I do this even with my poor voice; there's no better way to make a natural connection with your inner feel-ing. I would also advise any young musician to listen to recordings of some of the great singers of our century, such as Rosa Ponselle.

What an incomparable artist! I'm so grateful that you've singled her out.

STEINHARDT Listening to her recordings was a major musical event for me. Ponselle was like Schnabel in the kind of attention she gave to line and detail in a totally musical way.

The harmonic factor is, as I've said, important too. Once you view your melodic picture-graph in its harmonic context, some points of emphasis may need to be altered. A certain note in the phrase may want special emphasis even though it does not come at a melodic high point, because the composer has used an unusual or dramatic harmony.

Then there's the added factor of rhythm. Every melody has a natural lilt, a sense of give and take. I believe there's truth in the traditional concept of strong and weak bars within a phrase—for instance, the first and third bars may be stronger than the second and fourth.

Isn't there a risk of rigidity if one holds too closely to that principle?

STEINHARDT   Yes, of course; it shouldn't be adhered to dogmatically. The pattern of emphasis will certainly vary considerably depending on the music. But that doesn't negate the principle altogether. Even if the traditionally weak bar has been specially emphasized by the composer— say, with a sforzando that gives an offbeat stress—I still acknowledge somewhere inside me the presence of the strong bar.

A theme from Schubert—the second subject from the first movement of the G-major Quartet—might serve as an illustration of how these principles come into play. I don't mean to imply that someone, or even I myself, might not choose to play this music quite differently. My only purpose is to show the kind of thought process that I find helpful in interpretation.

This theme is really something of a miracle. Looking at the repetition of motif and the few notes involved, it's hard to imagine that it would get off the ground. And, I must say, one does sometimes hear it played almost as if it were more a rhythmic pattern than a melody. This is a pity, because Schubert has, in fact, created from these few notes one of the loveliest of melodies. Every curve of the line, every nuance, give color and meaning, and the interpreter must find the way to trace the design so as to convey that meaning.

The main thing is that the music should seem to "breathe"—to follow its natural sense of tension and release. In this respect it's important to establish just the right relationship between the first and second notes of the bar. I feel that the main emphasis should fall on the first beat—not the syncopation—after which there is a slight lift, and the syncopation subsides in a diminuendo. The syncopated note shouldn't be too clipped; in falling away from the main beat it settles into the line rather than interrupts it. Schubert sometimes places an unexpected accent on the third beat. These third-beat accents bring variety and charm and should, I think, be a shade stronger than the first beats.

Not only should the bars breathe but the whole phrase as well. This brings us to the question of "strong" and "weak" bars. The strong/weak pattern begins with bar 65 and alternates throughout, except in the case of bar 76, which acts as an additional strong bar to reinforce bar 75. My dynamic markings indicate this basic alternation of tension and release. However, the exact *degree* of strength and weakness is a matter of constant and subtle variation, which the interpreter will feel. As to bowing, I play on the string, changing the bow as the notes come—allowing a gentle lilt but being careful to maintain an overall continuity of line. The tempo is marked "Allegro molto moderato" and shouldn't be hurried.

Of course, beyond a certain point music making, in its subtlety and spontaneity, eludes analysis. I recall hearing Casals play in a performance of Schubert's E-flat-major Trio. His way of turning the phrases in the great theme of the slow movement was sheer magic. The analyzing, questioning young musician then took over within me, saying, "I don't want just to enjoy this; I want to understand *how* he does it." So I lay in wait for him when the same theme returns in the Finale. While there were main features of his interpretation that I could analyze, I still wasn't able to pinpoint just exactly why it was so extraordinary, just what made it so sublime.

One of the aspects of your playing that I greatly admire is the way you always convey a sense of cantabile when needed; there's never a feeling of "passage work." Take the thirty-second notes in the slow movement of Mozart's G-major Quartet [K. 387]. In your hands these always seem unhurried and have melodic shape. Some of the most beautiful passages of this sort in all the repertoire are the scalelike triplets in the second movement of Beethoven's Opus 59, No. 2, as in the following example:

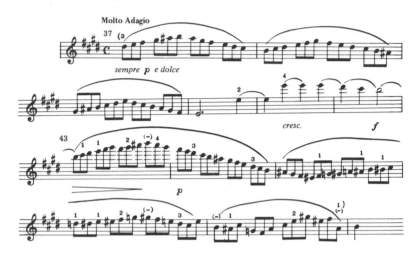

Would you comment on their interpretation?

STEINHARDT   How these simple notes are transfigured in Beethoven's hands! All these passages have a hymnlike quality; if rushed they would sound trivial. I try to play them with a natural, songful sonority: they're piano, not pianissimo—serene but not tremulous. Although a diminuendo is marked in bar 43, one still wants to keep the sense of the arc as the melody rises to the heights; I take a little extra time to sing on the high B. It's important that the line seem unbroken; one must look for fingerings that don't reveal all the shifts.

How do you divide the bowings?

STEINHARDT   I can't tell you exactly; I don't always do the same thing. It's not possible, of course, to sustain the bow over two bars. Sometimes I'll change the bow on an expressive note at the top of a phrase. To keep an illusion of a seamless line I would avoid always changing the bow on a main beat and vary the changes so that they don't always come where expected.

Of all violin passages in the quartet literature, nothing touches the interpreter's expressive capacity more deeply than the "beklemmt" section from the Cavatina of Beethoven's Opus 130. Szigeti wrote of this in A Violinist's Notebook,

"Not even the Four Thousand Bowing Exercises *of the estimable and indus-trious Sevčik have prepared one for these* parlando *up-bows."*

STEINHARDT   This passage is unique in all music. Rhythmically, the first violin's notes rarely coincide with any note in the accompanying triplets. It's a kind of planned chaos; it's like a man who's suddenly lost himself in the depths of despair, who's lost his bearings and is stumbling about, groping:

I begin almost inaudibly, without vibrato—truly *beklemmt* [stifled]—and then the vibrato gradually develops a little. In bar 46 we find that special Beethoven notation: two notes of identical pitch and time value slurred together. By means of both the left hand and the parlando up-bows that Szigeti mentions, I try to make this double impulse heard and *felt*. If anything, the second note comes as a reinforcement. One could call it a shudder or a cry. Even if he had written one note rather than two, I think one would know that something unusual is called for in the way of interpretation. You don't need a special notation; something has to speak to you from within to tell you what to do.

After twenty years' experience in the field, would you say that the process of quartet playing is in some ways related to one's personal development?

STEINHARDT   Oh dear . . . what can I say? Some of the qualities that have to be brought to bear in quartet playing are those that would serve one well in life. After all, I think most of us would like to have chances to lead in some respects while being content to follow in others. There's a harmonious balance in life when you can slip in and out of roles. Quartet playing provides that kind of variety. It requires great discipline, but there's a joy in any discipline in a creative field. There is something deeply satisfying in the economy of the quartet medium. To experience it, whether as listener or as player, brings a rare sense of wholeness. It's the most perfect unit of harmony one can have; all the voices are represented. With anything less there's something missing; with anything more there's an ornamentation, an extra richness. The quartet form is sparse, pure, and complete.

THE REPERTOIRE:
ASPECTS OF
PERFORMANCE

Let me begin by asking which works in your repertoire you find to be the most challenging.

TREE   I find playing Mozart the most difficult of all. There's such transparency of texture, such perfection of phrasing demanded, that you have to be careful not to overpower the music with personal idiosyncrasies. With Mozart I sometimes have the feeling that even if you sit down in the wrong way the audience will notice it. On the other hand, you don't want to be impersonal and uninvolved. Anyone who has read Mozart's letters will know that one shouldn't feel constrained in terms of emotional expression. And, indeed, what work is more romantic than the G-minor String Quintet?

DALLEY   The difficulty lies in finding just the right balance in performance. Mozart's art has an intangible quality that eludes precise definition. His music lingers halfway between the vocal and the instrumental. Take the Finale of the A-major Quartet [K. 464]. The theme seems almost a plaintive lament; you could imagine it coming from one of his operas. However, in the quartet context it takes on an intimacy and becomes a vehicle for compositional brilliance. Mozart's ideas often have a remote quality, as if they belong to another world. Think of the Finale of the D-major Quintet [K. 593]. It's a dance, and yet it's not a dance; it has a delicate character all its own. Even the minuets can be elusive—for example, the minuet from the G-major Quartet [K. 387], with its gentle, falling figure followed by chromatically rising phrases punctuated by expressive *fp* markings. These "in between" moods are the most difficult to capture. The Andante from K. 590 is a case in point:

The repetitive figure is so lovely that one is tempted to do too much with it, but its simplicity would then be destroyed. Perhaps in this movement it's enough if you just sit back and revel in its beauty.

On the other hand, with Haydn you can exaggerate certain elements of an interpretation and he won't be diminished by it. Mozart is more fragile; his musical language limits your possibilities. One is rarely bowled over by someone's interpretation of Mozart, but one normally hears Haydn played well; even when his music is approached quite differently by various artists the results are satisfactory. He has an earthy quality and is more accessible.

SOYER   We're always amazed at the ceaseless vitality of Haydn's musical mind. What tremendous variety there is in the quartets: glorious scherzos; profound slow movements which, especially in the later quartets, rival Beethoven; astonishing modulations anticipating Schubert!

Yet the once popular image of the simple, ever good-natured Papa Haydn is not entirely dispelled.

DALLEY   Haydn's musical language is direct, fresh, and natural. It's close to us, but it's not "simple."

TREE   I agree entirely, but I wouldn't want to slight Mozart in any way by comparison. I'd like to put a word in, too, for the early Mozart quartets—there are thirteen of them, all beautiful pieces—which are so rarely played.

SOYER   Alfred Einstein wrote of those early quartets, "Is spring only a foreshadowing of summer?"

STEINHARDT   If you keep that up, this will become a coffee-table book.

Dave, will you favor us further by discoursing on the work you find to be the most challenging?

SOYER   That would be the Schubert G-major Quartet—not only for its great length and instrumental difficulty but for its tremendous emotional and musical intensity. For forty-five minutes you're stretched drum-tight. There are passages in the first movement where he's hurling lightning bolts, and the energy and turbulence required seem to go beyond the capacity of the instruments. Even the tremolos in pianissimo must have great dramatic intensity. All four of us have to feel this together; sometimes it becomes almost unbearably tense. Such passages are then relieved by gentle, typically sweet Schubertian interludes of great simplicity. That juxtaposition in itself creates difficulties. The second movement has its share of stormy passages as well. The Scherzo is very delicate from the standpoint of ensemble, and the Finale, though musically lighter than the first two movements, is difficult to put together. Despite these problems, we adore playing the piece. It should be heard much more often. Performing it is, however, so strenuous that I doubt whether we would tour with it. The Budapest Quartet once did so and decided "Never again!"

TREE   Think of Schubert writing that piece at the age of twenty-nine— and in only ten days! There's no way of explaining such a miracle. If I had to choose my single favorite piece in the entire musical literature, it would be a work of Schubert, whether one of the last three quartets, the C-major Quintet, the Octet, or one of the great song cycles. One reads of the "heavenly lengths" of Schubert's works. Speaking rather selfishly from a performer's point of view, I think we're getting the best of the bargain. No Schubert work has ever felt long to us; it's a marvelous and exhilarating experience every time.

STEINHARDT   When playing one of these monumental Schubert works, I have the feeling that I'm setting forth on an epic journey. I feel that, too, when listening to the first movement of the "Great" C-major Symphony, with its mysterious trombone calls; one senses that Schubert is pacing himself for a long, long ride. In my heart of hearts I feel that there's no greater music.

Schubert didn't always write very idiomatically for strings. Yet, difficult as his quartets may be, I find them less challenging than Mozart's, for all the reasons that have been mentioned. People who come backstage after hearing us do a program that includes, for instance, Mozart and Bartók will often say, "Oh, that Bartók—what a hard piece it is!"— when we were, in fact, relieved to have gotten through the Mozart and to have come to the Bartók. Similarly, I feel more comfortable with late than with early Beethoven. In the Opus 18 quartets, as in Mozart, a crystalline quality, a perfection, is demanded; very little can be rough-hewn. Sometimes in the late quartets—for example, the Finale of Opus 131—one can really plow right into it. The *Grosse Fuge* is another example. From the instrumental point of view, you're painting on a large canvas in broad strokes, splashing on big blobs of color; and when you change colors the contrast is extreme. You have the wild frenzy of the first fugal section and then the Meno mosso passage, which is uniformly transparent and tender. The Opus 18 quartets, on the other hand, need an almost constant delicacy and precision. Yet these works—like those of Mozart—should always sound spontaneous, no matter how carefully they must be treated.

SOYER   Our feelings towards the Opus 18 quartets can be seen in the fact that when we recorded the Beethoven cycle we began with the large middle-period quartets, proceeded to the late quartets, and only finished with the Opus 18s.

DALLEY   In the "Razumovsky" quartets the whole sonority undergoes a change. The four parts are more nearly equal in prominence; the lower voices have more resonance. The melodies have a more sustained cantilena quality. There is more of a concerted sound—one could say a true string-quartet sound—fuller, richer than before.

TREE   It's fascinating to observe Beethoven's evolution throughout the quartets. When coming to the *Grosse Fuge* he seems to sidestep the nineteenth century altogether and plant his feet squarely in the twentieth century in terms of dissonance, sonority, and sheer abandon.

SOYER   A cycle of Beethoven's quartets is of unique interest; his spiritual development encompasses worlds. It's little wonder that the complete Beethoven cycle is in such demand; we're asked to play it at least once every season. There's a bottomless well of fascination in these pieces. New ideas seem to be coming up all the time. Much remains enigmatic—even some of the markings. There's a creative mystery that can never be entirely resolved.

Do you always play the quartets in the same order?

DALLEY   Yes, whenever we play the cycle in six concerts.★ On occasion

---

★ (1) Opus 127; Opus 18, No. 2; Opus 59, No. 3; (2) Opus 18, No. 3; Opus 95; Opus 132; (3) Opus 18, No. 4; Opus 18, No. 1; Opus 131; (4) Opus 74; Opus 18, No. 5; Opus 59, No. 2; (5) Opus 130; Opus 59, No. 1; (6) Opus 18, No. 6; Opus 133; Opus 135.

we've done it in five concerts, but that's very strenuous both for us and for the public. In deciding on the order in which we play the works we borrowed heavily from the Budapest Quartet version; their cycle was very well conceived. Because of its full, declamatory beginning, we consider Opus 127 the ideal work to open the cycle. And we conclude with the last quartet, Opus 135. The six-concert cycle allows us to include the short movement Beethoven wrote as a substitute for the *Grosse Fuge.* We use it to conclude Opus 130 because we feel that the *Grosse Fuge* can, if necessary, stand on its own, as it often does.

In general, how do you select your programs? I understand, Michael, that you're the quartet's "program chairman."

TREE   My role is really only minimal. I don't determine the basic programs; that's a joint effort on the part of all of us—and a rather painful effort it is. Each year we discuss what we're going to play the following season and sift through repertoire we haven't yet performed. We seldom agree, and each of us fights a personal battle for the works he loves best. We're always late in getting our choices to our manager, Harry Beall, who is, in turn, pressured by the concert organizations, which obviously want to know what we'll be playing. Having decided on our choices, we offer a selection of four or five different programs. Then my role begins; I act as liaison between our management and the quartet. Many times the concert-giving organizations will request changes; they may want a mixture from our programs or perhaps a work that we haven't listed. Whenever possible we accommodate them. However, somebody has to be there at the moment to explain that the organizers have unknowingly proposed three very long works, or that a program consisting of Haydn, Mozart, and Schubert isn't ideally balanced, or that we haven't the rehearsal time during that period to play a work not in our current repertoire, or that we can't play with a guest artist on a given date because we arrive in the late afternoon and won't have adequate rehearsal time before the concert. There are dozens of such situations, which require immediate responses. People are sometimes on a long-distance call with Harry while he phones me on another line. That's the nature of my being the so-called program chairman. And, of course, the boys always trust my judgment—or nearly always.

What criteria do you use for building programs?

DALLEY   Every year we offer one all-Beethoven program. We try to make the others interesting and well balanced. We're not known for striking new ground in playing avant-garde works, but we do offer two or three representative twentieth-century quartets each season. We generally play a classical work, a romantic one, and then something which, even if not contemporary, is somewhat outside the standard repertoire—perhaps Arensky, Chausson, Fauré, Wolf, Reger, Bruckner, Nielsen, Hindemith, Kodály. . . .

SOYER   There are quite a few great composers whose works in general are highly popular but whose quartets, though of outstanding quality, are strangely neglected. Schumann is an example. You'll hear the A-major "Clara" Quartet somewhat more often than the others, but all three are remarkable pieces.

STEINHARDT   We've found that Schumann's music, more than that of any other composer, seems to call for a personal interpretation, an improvisational approach. Everyone has wonderful thematic material to play, and one wants to treat it differently almost every time. Did you know that Schumann composed bridge passages so that all three quartets could be played without interruption? But he then decided against the idea and destroyed the music. I'd give anything to be able to see those passages.

How do you find the Schumann quartets from the standpoint of string writing?

DALLEY   The writing often seems quite pianistic. Nonetheless, Schumann wrote better for the quartet medium than Brahms, whose textures tend to be somewhat thick and orchestral. In Schumann the voices are laid out more openly, and this gives much more clarity. Although these works are difficult to play, they have a beautiful sonority.

STEINHARDT   Whatever problems there are in playing the Schumann quartets, they're not problems of the music itself; the essential musical quality is sublime.
    The Brahms quartets are performed more frequently. It's interesting: one often hears Brahms spoken of in terms of lush vibrato and rich sonorities, but it's important to avoid excess in this respect and to look for opportunities to bring transparency to his music. George Szell's performances provided a valuable insight. One might assume that Szell's dedication to clarity of texture would be chiefly beneficial to Mozart, but it also proved a revelation in the "romantic" repertoire.

SOYER   One composer who wrote beautifully for the quartet medium was Mendelssohn; but, like Schumann, he is unduly neglected. Such fine works as the A-minor Quartet [Opus 13] and the E-minor [Opus 44, No. 2] are heard all too rarely. Dvořák's chamber music—aside from the "American" Quartet—also falls into this category.

TREE   We rank Dvořák among the major composers. His melodic gift was outstanding. Although there's a lovely melancholic strain to his music, there's never breast-beating or a sense of self-pity; he's one of the healthiest and most natural of composers. Perhaps some of the finales don't quite meet the standard of the other movements, but this is a minor criticism considering the overall quality.

DALLEY   From the players' standpoint, Dvořák's choices of keys are sometimes problematic. When he writes in A-flat minor, as in the slow movement of the Quintet, Opus 97, intonation problems can arise, and the general sonority suffers somewhat from the lack of open-string resonance. I think Beethoven was more aware of the importance of the choice of key from the instrumental viewpoint. For example, in the "Heiliger Dankgesang" in the Lydian mode from Opus 132, the key of F allows him to utilize many open strings—above all, the cello's low C—which considerably enhances the sonorous quality of the whole ensemble.

SOYER   There's something of a trend these days away from the lesser-known "romantic" repertoire. As a result, many fine works are neglected: the Grieg Quartet, for example, a beautifully written piece that we're very fond of—vintage Grieg; or the Sibelius Quartet, *Voces Intimae*—its slow movement almost has the aura of late Beethoven. We're playing the Tchaikovsky D-major Quartet [Op. 11] this season; while the audiences seem to enjoy it greatly, some critics turn up their noses at it. This is mere snobbery. After all, we only commit ourselves to play works we believe in, and once we've performed a piece some forty times within a season, we're in a particularly good position to judge its qualities.

You frequently perform the Debussy and Ravel quartets.

STEINHARDT   Both are masterpieces. Since there's comparatively little French quartet literature, one often speaks of the two together; but they're quite different in character. While the Ravel may owe something to the Debussy—there are certain structural similarities—there's nothing truly imitative in Ravel's work. Some people prefer it, not because it's a better work but because it's more intimate, almost oriental in flavor.

The Debussy is highly dramatic; the opening is stormy and virile. As you see, one can't make any generalizations about a "French sound" or an "impressionistic atmosphere."

I once discussed Debussy's Pelléas et Mélisande *with Ernest Ansermet—a truly great interpreter of that work. He disliked performances in which one color continually melts into another; he stressed that the score should be treated boldly—with clarity and passion.*

STEINHARDT   Exactly. When playing either of these quartets you're telling a very detailed story; you need every color of the palette—not only pastels but primary colors. In fact, there's nothing more brilliant or afire in all the string-quartet literature than the beginning of the last movement of the Ravel Quartet or of the first movement of the Debussy.

What is your assessment of the quartet music of the so-called Second Viennese School?

DALLEY   We've played Berg's Opus 3 and his *Lyric Suite*. I would say that they're great in spite of themselves. They're overloaded with details that tend to get in the way of the essential musical message. It sometimes seems like a dissertation on how to utilize complicated motivic material. It's interesting to compare the Allegro misterioso of the *Lyric Suite* with the Prestissimo, con sordino of Bartók's Fourth Quartet. Both movements convey the same sort of mood—whispered, sporadic, fleeting— but Bartók is more successful, because he understands the limits of the language and knows just how much the listener can perceive. Nevertheless, Berg's works have a powerful emotional impact. The brevity of Opus 3 helps a good deal.

STEINHARDT   We've played Webern's Five Movements and Six Bagatelles—striking pieces. Of Schoenberg we've performed only the Second Quartet; I must confess that I'm not attracted to the third and fourth.

TREE   I find myself increasingly fascinated by his music—by the String Trio, for instance. I remember hearing the Fantasy for Violin and Piano—a doctrinaire twelve-tone piece—for the first time and not getting anything out of it. But after studying and performing the work I was able to appreciate it on its own purely musical terms.

SOYER   I consider *Verklärte Nacht* a masterpiece, and I find the Fourth Quartet to be a romantic, expressive work in its way. But, in general, my interest wanes when it comes to Schoenberg's twelve-tone music. The system seems limiting and somewhat pointless. The incessant harmonic tension tends after a while to take on a certain sameness, like one long diminished-seventh chord.

STEINHARDT   The twentieth-century composer whom I am most drawn to is Bartók. One of the attractions of his music is that though his writing is often atonal, there are—especially in his later works—tonal centers that offer contrast and relief. The dissonances become all the more poignant in that context.

The second movement of the Fifth Quartet is a beautiful example of this.

STEINHARDT   Yes indeed. I find the whole Fifth Quartet extraordinary. Its Finale is wild and anguished. When, towards the end, a simple diatonic folk tune is introduced, it's as if something has snapped, as if someone has suddenly been released from a state of torment and regressed into childhood. The Sixth Quartet, with its tragic motto-theme, is also a deeply affecting work.

TREE   I think there's the stamp of genius on all of the Bartók quartets— even the first, though it seems a little overlong for the material.

DALLEY   I believe the second has the best ideas; we all like it very much. I also have a special fondness for the third. It's an astringent work; but its very severity and brevity give it strength, like Beethoven's Opus 95.

STEINHARDT   One thing that sets the Bartók quartets apart, aside from their intrinsic merit, is their startling innovations in string writing. In that sense Bartók's quartets remind me of Beethoven's: rather than just following a logical evolution, they took a dramatic turn in a new direction. When I first heard the Bartók quartets—I was a teenager at the time—I knew I was in the presence of an extraordinary creative force, even if I didn't entirely understand it.

I feel that his innovations, which were very special at that time, are all still related to expression—unlike many contemporary works, where effect is often used for effect's sake.

DALLEY   I don't entirely agree. I admire Bartók for his courage and imagination, but I do think that some of the effects are tacked on. Nor are they all ideally calculated from the standpoint of effective string writing.

SOYER   The voicing of chords is sometimes unnecessarily problematic, as is the designation of certain notes to be played in extremely high positions on the lower strings. He often uses one string as a drone while simultaneously playing on another string, and this doesn't always sound to advantage.

STEINHARDT   Well, I don't agree with my colleagues. I find the writing for the most part wonderfully effective. Take the pizzicatos followed by glissandos; for me there's no gimmickry here, only heartfelt expression. In general, the fiddle writing is highly idiomatic—more so than in Brahms, Schubert, and sometimes even Beethoven.

You've referred to some quartet writing that almost seems to want to surpass the limits of the medium. What do you think of orchestral transcriptions of such works—for example, the Grosse Fuge?

TREE   When the *Grosse Fuge* is played by a string quartet, it's like scaling a mountain peak. At times it sounds rather strident—even unpleasant—deliberately so. What's wrong with that? By adding player upon player, by smoothing the edges and making it more agreeable, you eliminate the immediacy of the confrontation. When four players are solely responsible for maintaining their parts in a work of that magnitude, there has to be a greater sense of personal responsibility. There's also more room for spontaneity, for the unexpected. That's not to say that orchestral players aren't committed. But thirty or sixty string players cannot react like four. It's a different point of view.

SOYER   I agree. A great deal is sacrificed when that sense of struggle is lacking. I don't believe the *Grosse Fuge* was intended for orchestral performance.

DALLEY   My view may be considered heretical, but I'm not sure that Beethoven's concept of writing the *Grosse Fuge* for the quartet medium is successful. Yes, from the players' point of view there's a Herculean struggle, and that's most impressive. But I think that the material is ideally suited to a large mass of strings, particularly if the basses are used with discretion. I prefer something that sounds better, even if it's not totally authentic. I do feel, however, that some quartets aren't suitable for string orchestra. I recently heard a transcription of Beethoven's Opus 131 and didn't like it at all.

For me it's not a question of quartet versus orchestra; it's the interpretation itself that counts. Have you heard the Furtwängler recording of the Grosse Fuge? *It doesn't sound smooth at all but very rough indeed. You do have the feeling that you're scaling a mountain peak.*

STEINHARDT I admire that recording greatly. The transcription does work; it has tremendous power. While I prefer the original version, I think that Michael has some sort of ideal string quartet in mind. How many live up to that standard?

TREE The *Grosse Fuge* obviously presents an enormous challenge to any group that attempts to interpret it, string quartet or orchestra. I hate to take an anti-orchestral view of things; I'm not at all of that mind, believe me. I can't imagine the world existing without the great symphonic literature. But string-quartet music shouldn't be made to sound lush. The string-quartet medium is like the fine drawing of a master, and the moment you make something grandiose of it you tamper with the spirit.

STEINHARDT I do think, though, that some quartets lend themselves to orchestral transcription better than others: Smetana's *From My Life,* for example.

TREE Oh, I can't believe that, though I confess I haven't heard Szell's recording.

STEINHARDT It's charming, absolutely charming.

TREE But that, of all pieces . . .

STEINHARDT And the Verdi Quartet.

SOYER I can't imagine it.

As we seem to have reached an impasse, it might be an opportune moment to change the subject. May I ask what value you, as quartet players, place on having an extensive knowledge of the general repertoire?

SOYER You're greatly handicapped if you come to a work cold, without having a knowledge of the composer's idiom, of his language. Some time ago I heard a performance of the Janáček Violin Sonata which seemed impressive to me; I was sitting next to Rudolf Firkusny and told him my reaction. "Oh, no," he said, "there's not the right feeling for rubato. It's too literal a rendering of the score, and that's not the way it's meant to be played." That was interesting to me, as I had little knowledge of Janáček's music. Firkusny is, of course, Czech; he had known Janáček personally and was fully conversant with his music.

STEINHARDT When any one of us began to study our first Bartók work, we may have loved it, but there was an enormous strangeness to the whole thing. Now, however, when we play a Bartók quartet we've gained in understanding through having known all the violin pieces, the Music for Strings, Percussion, and Celesta, the Concerto for Orchestra, and many other works. We're all comfortable with the idiom.

TREE   The reverse is also true. Having played the quartets, we approach other music by the same composer with greater understanding. I often have occasion to teach the Bartók Viola Concerto. Much of the writing resembles that of his quartets; I make comparisons and quote relevant passages, and this proves helpful to those students who lack that frame of reference.

SOYER   When Horowitz studies a work of, say, Schumann, he looks through a great many Schumann pieces: not only the piano literature but songs, symphonies, chamber music, and concertos. Toscanini prepared in the same way. It's also helpful to be acquainted with the background from which the music sprang. Most of my students have no firsthand knowledge of middle-European folk music. That creates a problem when they have to play dance movements, minuets and scherzos of Haydn, Beethoven, or Schubert. All through their lives those composers heard country dances, Ländler, or gypsies playing. In America we have little exposure to that tradition. And, sad to say, it's now gradually disappearing in Europe. It's no longer easy to find a gypsy fiddler playing in a café.

TREE   We were speaking before of "the most challenging work." When you come down to it, every work is a challenge to be met on its own terms. One feels this each time one steps onto the stage. Sometimes a piece that seems comparatively easy to play poses the greatest problems. Take the "Malinconia" from Beethoven's Opus 18, No. 6:

If I had to audition a young quartet I would ask them to play the beginning of this movement. It demands the utmost in sustained ensemble playing. The mood must be there from the very beginning; the music should sound as if it's just lifted out of the air. The turns are always singing and expressive and yet are always *changing*—more rapid and dramatic in forte [bar 13], more yielding in piano.

To bring the breath of life to this simple yet eloquent piece is one of the hardest tasks a quartet can undertake.

A FIFTH PRESENCE

You have stressed the independence each of you maintains as a player. Yet time and again when you perform, a unity of conception does prevail, not only in a technical but in a spiritual sense—as it did last night in the ethereal slow movement of Schubert's "Death and the Maiden" Quartet. In the Finale some inexorable force seemed to be directing and shaping every bow stroke in that demonically propelled rhythm. At such times one feels something beyond four individuals; the whole becomes more than the sum of the parts.

DALLEY   It's true that there are occasions when we really do seem to feel and breathe as one player, and there have been moments when I've felt we've transcended everything we've done before. Much of it may be nothing more than the sheer science of quartet playing, but one would like to think that there is also some power at work which does enable one to scale new heights. That's becoming rather metaphysical.

TREE   At such times it may only be that we're succeeding in coming a little closer to the power of the music itself, to the greatness of the work at hand—to unlocking and releasing that power. I agree that when all's said and done, there is an element of the mystic in the process.

DALLEY   Such special moments occur rarely; that makes the experience all the more elusive. For instance, if you play tennis it requires a strong commitment to achieve a high general standard. But then to elevate your game the least little bit requires a commitment ten times greater than that which you've given before. You don't succeed in getting beyond that level very often, probably not more than a few times in your life, and when it happens, it occurs unexpectedly—of itself. You do feel almost as if a guiding hand were there to help you. In our quartet per-

formances these instances come from time to time for brief moments—
certainly not for an entire work. That would be something fearful. I'm
so mystified when it happens that I'm really the last person to explain it.

STEINHARDT   When a performance takes flight I feel as if all four personalities meet somewhere in the air—maybe two and a half feet above the
quartet.

Almost like a fifth presence . . .

TREE   A fifth presence? I cannot say. But something *is* going on; I can't
deny that.

DALLEY   Once, several years ago, during the "Heiliger Dankgesang"
from Beethoven's Opus 132, I felt that even though our playing wasn't
entirely free from blemishes, the overall performance had a special quality that we've never captured quite so well since. One couldn't explain it
from a technical standpoint; it wasn't that at all. I only felt that we were
coming close to the essence of what Beethoven had in mind when he
wrote the piece: that kind of hymnlike obeisance to a higher power. Our
performance of the rest of the quartet was comparatively unimpressive;
but I do think we truly sustained the mood throughout almost all of the
slow movement. And that's doubly difficult, not only because of its
length but because of a technical problem that can ruin any mood. A
few bars before the end there are a lot of open strings, which come just
when everything should be ascending, and if the strings are out of tune
it can be a real nuisance. I felt that all of us shared the same sense of
something special taking place.

SOYER   Of course, by its very nature such a movement demands that
we have a completely homogeneous sound. But, as John says, it's sometimes more than our attempt to make it so; everything becomes concerted and blended and propelled as if by itself. The music seems to take
over.

The music is playing you.

SOYER   Yes, that's a good way of putting it. It sounds a bit like Zen
Buddhism, but it does really seem like that. I must confess that sometimes while we're playing, I have the very weird sensation that someone
is looking over my shoulder. I'm a bit embarrassed to admit that. It's as
if some sort of presence is there watching me, or even watching the

whole quartet. Sometimes I sense Casals standing by my shoulder; sometimes it's Frank Miller, or even David Popper, the great cellist of the turn of the century.

Both Casals and Frank Miller played rather fatherly roles in your musical life.

SOYER   That they certainly did.

I hope they're looking on favorably.

SOYER   At those moments I think they are. Maybe they don't come when they're dissatisfied.

STEINHARDT   Whether or not they visit as apparitions, it's interesting to consider how the spirits of our mentors live on and are reborn in the individual player. It's a kind of crystallization or filtering through you of all the things that you have absorbed from others through the years—a mixture of ingredients that then takes on its own individuality.

It's clear that we ourselves can't accept all the credit for whatever good things there may be in a performance. If we're well enough prepared instrumentally, and open to the experience, we are, in a very true sense, only vessels through which the music passes; we have to acknowledge a force greater than ourselves.

Wouldn't it be only fitting for the Quartet to share its fee with that mysterious fifth presence?

STEINHARDT   An excellent idea. With that inducement it might come more often.

BEETHOVEN'S
OPUS 131

*Quartet No. 14
in C-sharp Minor*

First Movement

TREE Opus 131 occupies a unique place even among the greatest of Beethoven's works; it was, in fact, his favorite among his quartets. Playing it is an awesome experience. It's the longest nonstop work in our repertoire. Not only does one have to sustain the highest degree of concentration for forty minutes, but it's no small matter to maintain good intonation on instruments which over that length of time are bound to go out of tune, especially when we have to contend with a very warm stage. And all four instruments can go out of tune in different ways. We somehow have to cope with that.

Coming to terms with this work presents the interpreter with an enormous challenge. The fugal material of the first movement is of the utmost seriousness and grandeur. It is a mystical meditation and yet deeply human. There are places, such as the duet between the viola and cello [bars 73–79], which are tender beyond words. Despite the richness of feeling, the music always preserves an inward quality. We have to phrase expressively, yet always with dignity; we have to make ourselves worthy of the music if we can. So these are some of the thoughts that race through my mind at the very outset.

SOYER Of all the quartet literature, I have the deepest emotional response to this work. It has an unbroken power of expression—intense and yet restrained—until the tremendous release of the last movement. For me the first movement has a pervading tragic quality, a sense of foreboding; it's a magnificent prelude to all that's to come. It's fascinating to observe how Beethoven develops the two parts of the fugue subject independently as the movement evolves—in segments, in inversion, in diminution, in augmentation; the material sometimes appears simultaneously in three different time values. Yet one is never aware of technique for technique's sake. The whole movement seems to unfold naturally, almost like a song; and the performance must above all preserve a continuity, a sense of inevitability from beginning to end.

DALLEY   In general the writing is a model of contrapuntal clarity. The performer should, however, be conscious of those places where one voice has only a segment of the fugue subject while another will at the same time be stating it in its entirety. The segment should defer to the complete subject. One can discuss shadings and tempo, but in terms of balance it's basically quite clear-cut—like the *Grosse Fuge*.

TREE   It's rather difficult to find the ideal tempo. By qualifying his "Adagio" with "ma non troppo" and marking alla breve, Beethoven indicates that even though the material is extremely serious, it must flow.

DALLEY   Yet the "ma non troppo" shouldn't intrude upon the mood; the tempo mustn't roll along too quickly. On the other hand, if you take a tempo that's too slow, you may lose the sense of linear motion. Furthermore, many problems will ensue when it comes to sustaining the long bow strokes.

STEINHARDT   The opening statement is a dramatic event, not only because one is announcing the fugue subject but because the motif of the first two bars is used in later movements as well:

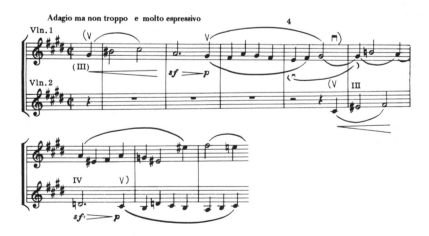

Intonation is a prime expressive factor. The leading note, B sharp, has a magnetic attraction towards the C sharp. There's also a relationship between the upbeat G sharp and the fourth note, A, although they're separated by a full bar. I draw the G sharp ever so slightly upwards and return to that pitch after leaving the A. However, owing to the slow speed at which the notes move, the semitones shouldn't be exaggeratedly narrowed. As for quality of sound, I personally don't hear a normal big, healthy violin tone here. The character is mournful and melancholy and needs a purer, more ethereal timbre. I begin with an almost colorless vibrato—thin, slow, and uncommitted. As the crescendo develops, I increase the speed of the vibrato but not its width. The sforzando should emerge from the crescendo in a natural way and come with just the right degree of strength. It's deeply expressive—very intense but not harsh—and when it arrives it's not just a pinpoint; it must be spread out in time. I maintain the full intensity of the vibrato for at least the length of a quarter note. After the opening two bars, which seem so anguished, the subsequent quarter-note figure proceeds with an uncanny calm. I play these notes quietly, avoiding a rise and fall in dynamics. The printed slurring almost invites an unwanted accent on the G sharp in bar 4. I prefer to sustain the bow until after the beginning of the G sharp and disguise a bow change on it after the second violin enters. If the hall is terribly dry and I feel I need a shade more sound, I might be tempted to change the bow on the E at the beginning of the fourth bar.

DALLEY I prefer to begin my statement of the fugue subject in first position, because the E sharp and the F sharp will correspond to the D-string timbre of the first violin. My sforzando D then gains in relief when played on the G string. I play the eight quarter notes on one up-bow in accordance with the indicated slur; it's uncomfortable to end up at the frog, but one has to live with it. If Arnold does change bows in the course of his quarter notes, I'll bow my quarters similarly.

TREE You may recall that I spoke of my solo statement of the fugal subject in the Finale of Beethoven's Opus 59, No. 3 as being the easiest of the entrances, although the most exposed. Now the opposite occurs; mine is the third entrance, and I don't have the luxury of shaping things just as I might wish:

This is a moment of true concerted playing where we try to find exactly the same quality of vibrato, degree of crescendo, and bow speed. (However, this isn't to say that the overall character of the movement may not differ slightly from performance to performance. At one time it may be somewhat more agitated; at another, more meditative.) The viola statement differs from the others in having a crescendo indicated in its third bar [bar 11]. To gain a bit more sound I feel justified in changing the bow at the beginning of bar 12, but although this is the climactic point of the crescendo, I avoid an overt accent on the bar line; the writing calls for an extremely linear, legato approach.

DALLEY   In bars 10–11 the crescendo of the violins precedes that of the viola. In order of importance come the viola with the complete fugue subject, the second violin with a condensed version of the subject, and the first violin with its accompanying notes. The dynamics should be gauged accordingly.

SOYER   The cello entrance runs the risk of being covered by the other voices.

I look for a rather substantial, firm-core sound—more an intensity of sound under the bow than a vibrato intensity. At the beginning of the movement when Arnold states the subject by himself, he comes down to piano just where marked. But if I were to do that, the quarter notes would be lost. I therefore sustain enough tone for the whole subject to be heard and only really arrive at piano at the end of bar 16, two bars later than written. It's a question of judging at the moment just how much volume you need to come through the texture.

As for intonation, each voice maintains the basic sense of harmonic direction that Arnold has described. However, apart from the initial statement, the upbeats have to be considered in reference to the given harmony. This would apply to my first C sharp [upbeat to bar 13], which initially strikes the ear as being the bass to the harmony and thus shouldn't be raised in pitch. However, my subsequent C sharp [bar 14] is perceived as being part of the cello melody and could therefore be played just a hair's breadth higher.

STEINHARDT   As the other voices enter, I have to make choices note by note. First of all, I must get out of the way immediately; yet I have to fill in the harmony in such a way that the other voices are adequately supported. I must also remain alive to the harmonic implications. For instance, at bar 14 my A sharp is unexpectedly carried over in a suspension. This is a case where rather than making an actual crescendo I would color the note with more vibrato, so that it lights up for a brief instant without intruding on the fugal entry.

SOYER   Despite the general clarity of texture, there are certain passages where one has to help out a little. For instance, in bar 21, just as the first violin reaches the top of its crescendo, the cello enters in the low register in piano with the leading voice:

If that entrance is to be heard clearly, some sleight of hand is necessary. The first violin has to hedge a bit and withdraw just a little from the conclusion of the crescendo, and the cello will have to accentuate its upbeat and then drop down immediately to piano before beginning its crescendo. In this way the entrance stands out in relief.

TREE　　Later in the movement the second violin and the viola have a similar dialogue. These passages may look beautiful on paper, but to make them heard properly we as players have to do things that seem momentarily to contradict what's on the page. However, if we annotate the upbeat with a *mp* and an accent, this shouldn't be interpreted in an exaggerated way; it's purely an acoustical matter.

SOYER　　All editions of the full score indicate that the cello should play D natural in bar 24. However, the cello part in the Peters edition gives D sharp, which seems more "logical," as it's in keeping with the intervals of the first bar of the fugue subject. I prefer the D natural. It's less expected; it alters the character for an instant—just a subtle change of mood—and has an unusual beauty.

DALLEY　　It's difficult to know where to change bows in this movement. One wonders whether certain slurs were set down by Beethoven as only a general indication of legato or whether they were meant to show exactly where a phrase begins and ends. The slurs often have an expressive connotation. For instance, in bars 21–26 the fugal motif appears in the form of a dialogue; the slurs are mostly very short. The dialogue builds to a climax at bar 27, after which the parts flow in a more concerted manner. At this point Beethoven places slurs over groups of four bars, which suggests a greater serenity:

STEINHARDT　　One can help to preserve a sense of unbroken line here by not always changing the bow in the same place during the sequence.

SOYER　　We envisage the phrasing in subdivisions beginning where the leaps occur—on the second quarter of each bar. This idea has much general validity. For example, in the Bach suites, where there are no dynamic markings to guide one, a break in the line might intimate that some phrasing is intended. In this case we don't necessarily change the bow on the second beat; the phrasing is more imagined than real—but imagined enough to produce a tiny inflection.

DALLEY   Although a crescendo is marked at bar 34 in all parts, it should be remembered that the viola has the leading voice:

In bars 43 and 44 there's a wonderful modulation from G-sharp minor to E-flat minor. We make a diminuendo and find a new color by using a paler vibrato:

STEINHARDT   There are many long crescendos in this movement, and it's wise to plan in advance how each may best be gradated. At bar 50 the cello has the leading voice, which culminates (at the double bar) in a more important statement of the theme than that of the first violin.

However, the cello is in its low register here, and can easily be covered by the violin playing on its bright E string. The violinist can help in this passage by giving the *illusion* of a crescendo, more through an increase in left-hand intensity than in actual volume.

DALLEY   When, in bar 55, the eighth notes replace the quarters as the basic unit of motion, there may be a tendency to play faster. We counteract this tendency by slightly pulling back—which actually increases the sense of power. Here, all the parts are of equal importance, all are related to the subject; and in coming together they produce great strength. In bars 63–64 the quarter-note motion is gradually resumed, and we release the tempo again:

STEINHARDT   At bar 67 the last six notes of the fugue subject emerge in a wonderful dialogue in major:

This passage is serene but radiant. It shouldn't sound fragile but should sing in a very natural way; we play mezzo piano here.

SOYER   It's quite possible that Wagner had these phrases at the back of his mind when he wrote *Parsifal*. His "faith" motif is very similar in melodic shape as well as in atmosphere, and he even gives it similar contrapuntal treatment. He revered Beethoven's string quartets and wrote about Opus 131 in a most poetic way.

The two lower voices then take up the dialogue:

Since I play in a higher register than the viola, I look for a quality of sound that's light and limpid—expressive but not covering.

DALLEY   At bar 83 we retain the printed slurring, although it's rather difficult to sustain two bars in one bow:

We do, however, have a kind of built-in elasticity. If the person playing the lead voice feels inhibited by a bowing at any time, he has the option of changing bows and allowing himself a little more ease in playing. We all have to be aware of this and go with him. However, in such a passage one must be rather careful. Too many bow changes can easily produce lumps in the line and raise the dynamic level.

SOYER   From bars 99 to 107 the fugue subject is played in augmentation by the cello:

However, this statement may not be easily perceived in its entirety, particularly as the three upper voices have quicker note-values. Clear articulation of each note in the cello part will help in asserting the theme's identity.

DALLEY   We can help, too, by adapting our crescendo to the sonority of the cello, which here, in its deepest register, is pitted one against three. The augmentation of the theme brings a great consolidation of energy. From there on, everything flows inevitably to the conclusion.

SOYER   It's interesting to note in bars 113–115 that Beethoven wrote B sharp rather than merely an open-string C. This was most audacious for the time.

People probably wondered whether the cello could play such a note. From the standpoint of intonation the B sharp, as the leading note to C sharp, should be slightly higher than the C. If I'm feeling virtuous I'll place my first finger right next to the nut, just enough to raise the pitch a fraction.

TREE   This is one of those passages where we think of the sforzandos as progressively gaining in intensity, the final one [in bar 116] being the climax of the phrase. One really reaches the outer limits of music here; one can't play with enough passion or involvement.

SOYER   The bass is very important in the final bars:

The double-stops in the viola and cello, giving the tonic and dominant together, convey tremendous strength.

TREE   The slurs binding several notes present a textual problem rather like the conclusion of the Cavatina. A decision has to be made as to where separations are intended. From the previous bars we take it that the feeling of syncopation is a predominant feature of the passage, and we thus change bows here on the syncopated notes. However, one should avoid too obvious a separation; it's really no more than a pulsation.

STEINHARDT　No matter how many times we've played this movement it always seems a new experience. The intellectual control of the writing is remarkable; all the parts fit together like a fascinating puzzle. At the same time, there seems to arise from it an almost tangible spiritual quality. I don't know exactly how to describe it; it's never quite the same. Much depends on the conditions under which we're playing and the mood of the moment. Perhaps we're speaking here of that undefinable "fifth presence."

Second Movement

DALLEY　The modulation from one movement to another is beautiful in its starkness and simplicity:

It's important to sustain the mood over this transition and to avoid starting the second movement too abruptly.

STEINHARDT　The sonority at the end of the last note of the first movement—the C sharp—should carry over to the D. If you have no more than a single hair of the bow on the string, you should continue like that. What does change is the kind of vibrato you use to get at the character—a vibrato of greater width.

SOYER   The new movement is immediately more lively; it's light, airy, elegant, and scherzolike. But I sense as well an element of sadness, a bittersweet quality. And, of course, the octave leap becomes a motif that is used several times in the course of the movement.

TREE   One often hears this movement played too fast. The marking is "Allegro molto vivace." Allegro, yes—but "molto vivace" indicates the character; it's not a tempo marking.

STEINHARDT   And the character is dancelike. I wouldn't be surprised if, consciously or not, Beethoven derived this material from some sort of folk music.

DALLEY   The second violin is largely responsible for setting the tempo; I have to act as intermediary between the first violin and the others and establish the pulse. The syncopations should be played very lightly— only a little impulse, followed by a diminuendo.

TREE   The melodic line needs to be gently caressed. Here's a case where we would not want to play the eighths later than written—they should never sound like sixteenths; the rhythm shouldn't be angular and jerky.

STEINHARDT   The phrasing is influenced by the pattern of alternating strong and weak bars. I think of the first bar and a half as an upbeat, with the strong beats falling on the second and fourth complete bars. But at bar 5, which one would normally expect to be a "weak" bar, the melodic line traces a little rainbow, implying a slight rise and fall in dynamics, and this gives an unusual charm to the phrase. All these nuances are, of course, very subtle. The indication "un poco ritard" should also be interpreted subtly, so as not to break the flow of the line. It was almost unnecessary for Beethoven to designate this. One should, in any case, feel the natural rounding off of the phrase. When seeing such a marking, one has a tendency to overreact, to think that because the composer took the trouble to put it in black and white, you've got to *do* something. The fermatas that come later in the movement should also be no more than a brief lingering.

TREE   The eighth notes are a thread reappearing throughout the movement; we constantly vary them in length and attack:

For example, in bar 13, when I join the cello, Dave and I will bounce the bow almost like tapping a little drum. It's a rather playful stroke; the accent falls on the downbeat, and the following two eighths come in a rebound. The figure retains its contour as the crescendo mounts. But then as we reach the climax of the crescendo at bar 17 I will shift gears and match the second violin; by that time we'll be playing a much longer spiccato stroke. These differences should occur imperceptibly, without people thinking, "Ah, listen to that; they've suddenly changed the length of their bow stroke."

DALLEY   Balance is a delicate matter here. The figure of three eighths can easily become too aggressive as the crescendo develops; it risks obliterating the melody.

SOYER   At bar 17, just when one would expect the crescendo to carry through to the forte, Beethoven inserts a diminuendo followed by a subito forte. The changes of nuance are lightning fast, and the effect is startling. These unusual dynamic markings must be respected here and at all the reappearances of this figure—bars 20–22, for example.

When considering the intonation of the semitone C sharp–D in bars 44–48, one should remember that the C sharp is the root of the harmony. Thus it shouldn't be drawn upwards towards the D. On the contrary, the D should be drawn downwards towards the C sharp:

At the upbeat to bar 49 the octave motif comes again; a slight articulation helps give it character.

STEINHARDT   At bar 60 the mood becomes more robust. Again we find an almost violent contrast in dynamics from bar to bar:

DALLEY   In contrast to the linear quality of the first violin, the lower voices play almost percussively; it's a very insistent figure, done in the lower part of the bow with up/down strokes. One should take care to sustain the quarter notes a shade longer than the eighths.

STEINHARDT   The sforzandos coming on the offbeats [bars 66–69] have something a little grotesque and devilish about them. They need to be extremely pointed; a sudden quickening of vibrato will help set them in relief.

DALLEY   At bar 74 the mood suddenly becomes lyrical:

The dialogue between the first and second violins can easily sound too clipped. Each of us will take just enough time for the upbeat to sing.

SOYER   The ensemble between the first violin and the cello can be tricky at the poco ritardando:

Some visual contact helps; I'll watch Arnold's left hand. Once the tempo is re-established in bar 96, things are less problematic.

TREE   Sometimes respecting the original slur turns out to be easier than adopting a more "comfortable" bowing. We play bars 114–117 in one bow rather than changing somewhere in the middle of the passage and risking an accent; the line remains unbroken:

STEINHARDT   Starting at bar 173 we have one of those "look ahead" passages where the crescendo mark shouldn't tempt you to be too loud too soon:

There are seven and a half bars before the *f* and another two before the *ff*. In bar 175, where the unison begins, we drop down to piano; this makes it easier to pace the crescendo. Then, having arrived at forte, we make a quick diminuendo in bar 182 to set the *ff* off more dramatically. Beethoven may be turning over in his grave, saying, "You fools, that's not what I meant; you're making my music too orderly."

TREE   As ever in unison passages, decisions have to be made as to the extent to which certain notes will be played with expressive intonation.

This is one of those moments when even we have to agree on everything! Everybody takes care to shift quickly so that no glissando is heard anywhere; it should sound almost pianistic.

DALLEY   From the second half of bar 176 to bar 180 the middle voice is doubled and thus tends to take on too much prominence; either the second violin or the viola should underplay a little. This is often a consideration in such passages. The slur extends over five bars. We stagger the bow changes to enhance the legato and the power of the crescendo. If this bowing is well executed, the differences aren't heard. The next two slurs (in bars 180 and 182) both begin in the middle of the bar. After the long phrase of five bars, the sense of syncopation should be emphasized at these points, as it brings a welcome variety to the phrase structure.

TREE   In the figure of two eighths at bar 185 the second note can sound limp without good articulation; the bow speed and release are as important as the attack:

SOYER   Towards the end of the movement the elongation of note values and the series of rests give, of themselves, an impression of slowing down; no further ritardando is needed:

We find here an enigmatic marking: "*p*" followed in turn by "mezza voce" and "*pp*." Now, what does "mezza voce" mean in that context? If we take it literally as "half voice," it would imply a higher dynamic level than piano—something in the nature of *mp* or *mf*. Or does it imply a decreased dynamic level, somewhere between *p* and *pp*? But in that case why didn't Beethoven simply write "più piano"? We've never resolved this question. For the present, we interpret the "mezza voce" in the latter way: coming down in volume. But I still suspect that the opposite is true and it's meant to come up in volume just before the final pianissimo notes.

DALLEY   The performance of this movement should convey effortlessness, fluency, and continuity. But, in fact, it takes a considerable effort within the quartet to achieve that result.

Third Movement

TREE   The Allegro moderato takes on a very sturdy rhythmic character—almost marchlike.

The two opening notes should have a feeling of grandeur. We play them martelé, using almost the whole bow; this is a case where the dots imply no more than a separation. The brief offerings of each player have something of a solo character. Though playful, they shouldn't sound timid.

SOYER   Nor should they trail off in diminuendo. One must keep in mind the continuity of the overall line. Since the second forte notes [bar 4] come at a higher level, we play them with increased emphasis.

TREE　We used to prepare for the adagio with a slight ritardando in the cello, but now we play the passage exactly as marked, with an abrupt change of tempo:

The viola's first eighth note belongs to the previous phrase; there's a comma, and then the whole character changes. Again, the dots don't imply that the notes should be short. These eighths are warm and expressive. I imagine them being sung—each note having a word that needs clear enunciation.

STEINHARDT　The little cadenza beginning in bar 8 should have an extemporaneous feeling. It rises in arcs; I give the highest note [the C sharp in bar 9] just a little extra time:

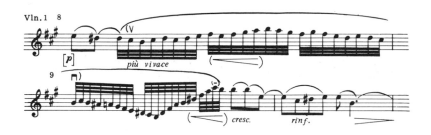

There's an adage that if you want a passage to sound fast, it's better to play it a little slower, but cleanly. Speed overkill is, in any case, not the point of the passage; it has warmth and charm.

SOYER　The final chord, though forte, should have a dolce character; Beethoven seems to imply this by including the forte in a legato slur and by leaving out the first violin:

This chord makes a bridge over to the Andante.

Fourth Movement

STEINHARDT   I give the lead, but then I follow the pizzicato of the cello; it's really up to Dave to establish the tempo. The sound of the pizzicato is precise; bowed entrances in a quiet passage are fuzzy by comparison.

SOYER   In marking "Andante ma non troppo" Beethoven implies a tempo that's flowing, but not too briskly. A little too fast and it sounds trite; a little too slow and it becomes heavy. To help me feel just the right degree of motion, I sometimes think ahead to a bar filled with notes of shorter duration—from the first variation, for example. The tempo is maintained without change until the Più mosso [bar 65].

   In all the quartet literature I can't think of another variation movement that has such tremendous scope, its only possible rival being the slow movement of Opus 127. But Beethoven treats these two movements quite differently. In Opus 127 the variations retain a closer relationship to the theme, while in Opus 131 they're dealt with more freely. Although rooted in the harmonic basis of the theme, each variation has a melodic and expressive character quite its own, sometimes seemingly remote from the original material. Elements of a decidedly rustic character are unexpectedly placed side by side with the sublime, yet everything sounds inevitable in its context. Beethoven often bases his miraculous creations on very simple material, and this is an example. The fact is that it's nothing much of a tune.

TREE   Objection! This is one of the most inspired melodies in all Beethoven. You won't find a lovelier tune. It has a Schubertian quality.

STEINHARDT   The sonority should be unforced, neither too loud nor too soft, like the natural sound of your voice if you were singing to yourself—quiet yet full. It helps to use a rapidly moving bow. The theme begins without a downbeat—a feature retained in several of the variations. There's a gentle gravitation to the second beat, reminiscent of such dances as the chaconne and the sarabande. The last note of each violin figure should always be sung through; the phrase should be handed on effortlessly. We arrange the bowings so that the melodic fragments answer one another down-bow/up-bow.

TREE   Beethoven could easily have given the whole line to one violin or the other. Rather than a monologue he chose a dialogue—a dialogue between two kindred souls, perhaps, but still a dialogue.

STEINHARDT   I'm not necessarily pleased when someone tells us, "Oh, it sounded as though only one instrument were playing!" We do a disservice to music if there aren't differences in the grain of each player. This isn't to say that we play this passage in an anarchical way; we listen closely to each other but allow ourselves to react spontaneously.

DALLEY   We often play the theme differently from one performance to another. I sometimes treat the second bar as a reinforcement of the first, sometimes as an answer coming more softly. In the fourth bar I may on occasion make a little crescendo, and once the phrase is committed that way, Arnold has to respond accordingly when playing his A in the fifth bar.

STEINHARDT   I usually go over to the E string for that A, as it brings more clarity and openness of expression. The hairpins are, however, more in the left hand than in the right. And, of course, John responds to what I do. There's a creative give and take.

DALLEY   The last two sixteenths in bar 8 and the first eighth in bar 9 conclude the previous phrase and should be played in diminuendo. After a breath the theme begins on the quarter-note A:

Here in the low register it's necessary to give more tone. I imagine for the moment that I'm playing the viola. Sometimes we play the theme very simply over the first eight bars and give more variety of nuance when it's repeated. Or we might reverse the order and play it more simply the second time. A purist might be horrified, but that's the way we are.

TREE   A satisfying interpretation of the first variation depends very much on the execution of the thirty-second notes which appear in figures such as the following:

Here two principles are at work: finding the natural rhythmic vitality by playing the thirty-second notes a shade later than written, and enhancing the clarity of articulation by making a diminuendo just before the thirty-second notes. The left hand should be as vital as possible; all the short notes need vibrato.

SOYER   The groups of sixteenths in the first violin and the cello provide a lyrical contrast in this variation. In bars 44–45 I phrase as follows:

At bar 63 I lead the ensemble. We articulate the bow lightly rather near the point, without too much nuance in the line itself:

TREE Arnold makes a slight ritardando just before the Più mosso. This is a place where the second violin leads. John and I have to establish the new tempo while playing a very precise stroke. A little telepathic understanding is useful here, and it certainly doesn't hurt to have played the piece many times together.

DALLEY We play the eighth notes very short and bright—all up-bow—using the collé bowing of which I've spoken. This stroke is also helpful for the double-stops; one can more easily catch and release both notes. We give equal stress to each beat rather than follow the nuances of the solo voice; we resist the temptation to phrase "musically."

STEINHARDT After the serene opening of the movement this variation's dancelike character is quite startling. I don't mean to be irreverent, but I'm almost reminded of a tango. Both in its texture and its simplicity this variation is reminiscent of the middle section of the second movement of Opus 132. In contrast to the regularity of the accompanying eighths, the melodic line needs contour:

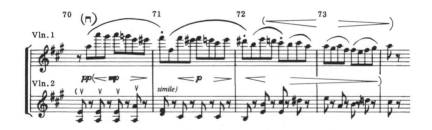

Bars 70 and 71 each have a little arc, but in bar 71 the whole dynamic level comes down just a bit. I would then give more tone in bar 72, followed by a gradual diminuendo over two bars. (Alternatively, in keeping with the upward movement of the second-violin line, one could make a crescendo into bar 73 and only then begin the diminuendo.) Expressive intonation is called for, and as one is playing up in the stratosphere, the semitones are extremely narrow.

DALLEY One has to be careful not to confuse the melodic and rhythmic elements. In bar 77 my first note concludes the melodic figure and should be played gently and slightly sustained; the next three eighths are immediately played with the collé stroke as before:

In bar 76 the interval of the fifth [E–B] can be dealt with either by playing both notes on the D string or by crossing strings. If Dave has made a rather bold crescendo in his previous phrase, I might respond to it by playing with less tone and simply cross over to the A string. On the other hand, if he's made very little crescendo, I would probably stay on the D string and make an expressive slide. This is a small example of how allowing yourself the option of changing fingerings contributes to spontaneity in performance.

SOYER In bars 78–81, like Arnold before me, I phrase the melodic eighth notes in a series of arcs, at first coming up above the dynamic level indicated and then gradually subsiding as the phrase descends:

SOYER At bar 82 I begin again in piano to build a long crescendo:

TREE   Here Beethoven gives the viola the role of two instruments. He wants to expand the quartet into a quintet! As the crescendo develops, I'll begin to sneak in different bowings—first of all, down/up to give more importance to the downbeats, and then, from bar 84, all down-bows for increased emphasis. In keeping with our idea of allowing a series of sforzandos to develop in intensity, we'll begin at the second note in bar 86 a little less than forte, the sforzandos being expressed mostly by the left hand:

As our crescendo develops, the sforzandos retain a singing quality, until, at the climax of the passage [bar 89], they become brusque and angular and we attack every entrance from the air. This passage is repeated immediately afterwards. We then make even more crescendo and come to a yet greater point of intensity.

STEINHARDT   As John has already mentioned, octave passages tend to sound more in tune when the upper voice—in this case the first violin—doesn't dominate. We find, too, that an increase in bow speed on the sforzandos helps them gain in definition. The next variation is again extremely daring. After such interlocked quartet writing the voices are now exposed nakedly. They carry on a dialogue as at the beginning of the movement, but without accompaniment:

TREE   The timing of the cello entrance needs attention. If the first note is played too late, it might be misinterpreted as a downbeat falling on the third beat of the bar. Yet if it comes too early, the entrance may seem precipitous.

SOYER   With Beethoven, "dolce" has an encouraging, not a retiring, connotation: it implies "singing" or "expressively." He also adds the unusual indication "lusinghiero," meaning "coaxing." Since the sixteenth notes here have melodic emphasis, we don't play them late and quick, as we would in a passage that has more rhythmic élan.

DALLEY   On the other hand, the sixteenths shouldn't be lazy; they mustn't degenerate into sounding like the last part of a triplet—all of which is to say that they're best played just as written, but very well articulated by the left hand.

SOYER   We follow the line of the phrase with a little rise and fall in intensity; we then change the bow on the bar line, giving a slight stress to the appoggiatura. Using more bow also enhances the singing quality. However, these nuances are very slight. It's important not to let the ends of the phrases drop off in diminuendo; the two instruments have to build one melodic line. These dialogues—between viola and cello, and then between the two violins—should have something of an improvisatory quality. They offer you considerable latitude to shape your part in a personal way.

DALLEY   For example, in bar 107, when answering Arnold's phrase, I may, if I wish, match his D-string color by remaining on the D string myself. But if I want to give more intensity to my response, coming, as it does, one tone higher, I'll go over to the A string:

These violin nuances, however, depend on what the viola and the cello have done before us. Sometimes they get carried away and make a great deal of their crescendos, in which case we violins respond by playing in a more understated way.

TREE   The second half of this variation is entirely different in character from its first half. I find this enigmatic passage extremely beautiful:

SOYER   There's a tendency to accompany this change of character with a quickening of pace. But one should hold back the reins here; a unity of tempo must be maintained throughout each variation.

TREE   We play the rising quarter notes espressivo, the dots not being too short; this crescendo has a longing—yes, coaxing—flavor. The descending eighths are more playful, the dots now being shorter; the bow, however, remains on the string. After the *sfp,* these eighths seem to be telling us that things aren't as portentous as they seemed. We hold back very slightly before the *sfp;* it's better to err in that direction than to fall into the note. One must also be careful that the *sfp* isn't too harsh; it's an expressive accent. This whole passage needs vital left-hand articulation.

STEINHARDT   Just after the *sfp* has subsided, one can warm up the vibrato again so that the note gains in intensity as it carries the phrase over the bar line. Each entering voice has to contend with the reverberation of the previous voice's *sfp,* so one must articulate each entrance clearly and then drop immediately to piano before building the crescendo. I would suggest making a plan to vary the intensity of these crescendos; they shouldn't all arrive at exactly the same level. For instance, in bar 122 the first violin might make only a slight crescendo, in bar 124 a little more crescendo, and in bar 126 a crescendo that somehow takes the huge leap into account. This can be done by combining more intensity of sound with a slight hesitation before the high note:

Of the two crescendos in bars 128 and 129, I hear the second as the less strong; it consists of only a half bar and prepares the mood for the Adagio. The last four eighths in bar 129 have no dots over them and are of a singing character.

SOYER   The transition into the wonderful Adagio with its unusual light, high voicing is particularly lovely:*

As we cross the double bar we try to have a little more motion, the eighth being a shade faster than the previous quarter. The second violin and cello set the tempo with their syncopation.

STEINHARDT   A common unit of beat between the variations may tend to create monotony. We like to feel here that the tempos are not connected—that we really set off in a new direction. We're passing from

* Beethoven's original notation is preserved here: in accordance with the custom of his time, cello passages in the G clef are indicated an octave higher than actual pitch.

common time to $\frac{6}{8}$, and although the new tempo is Adagio, it's a kind of dance, albeit a very slow one.

SOYER   We look for a transparent sound and keep the sixteenths moving towards the bar line without rhythmic self-indulgence. Although we change bow in the middle of the bar, we do so as discreetly as possible.

DALLEY   In anticipation of the second-violin pizzicato chord in bar 131, it's helpful to play the last two bowed notes right at the frog, so that the hand is close to the string. It's also useful to prepare the left hand in advance. When playing these two B's, one can simultaneously place the first finger on the D string, where it will be ready for the E in the pizzicato chord. As usual in pizzicato, the dynamic level should be raised. The upper note must sound as clearly as possible; vibrato is indispensable.

SOYER   One should remember that the cello's pizzicato note, though sforzando, is not actually forte, since the general dynamic level is piano.

TREE   The expected treatment would have been simply to fill in the bar with a lovely cantabile accompaniment, but we have instead this brusque interruption coming out of nowhere. The pizzicato in the cello is Brueghel-like in character: a rather poorly clad country fiddler decides to make his presence known.

STEINHARDT   The cello doesn't sound so poorly clad to me. It can resonate splendidly on its pizzicato, while the violin pizzicato sounds particularly ineffective in the upper register. In bar 141 I've sometimes experimented by playing only the upper and lower notes and omitting the middle E.

It's unorthodox, but at least it allows you to make use of the resonance of the open A string. As mentioned before, it helps the pizzicato to use a quick motion in releasing the strings.

DALLEY   In bars 142–145 one must consider the role of short segments in the overall line:

The second-violin figures in bars 142 and 143 both conclude their respective phrases; each has an implied diminuendo, while the first-violin figure arches over the bar line. But in bar 144, the two violins join together in building the line, and a diminuendo would be inappropriate. (The first sixteenth note in this bar is not part of the melody and shouldn't be stressed.) It was often Beethoven's practice—as in this variation—to alternate his dynamic markings between sets of hairpins and the written indications "cresc.–dim." The latter seem to imply a stronger shaping of nuance. The hairpins can be thought of more as an increase in intensity than in volume. It's important to observe these distinctions and also to resist the temptation to make a marked rise and fall in those passages for which no special nuances are indicated. Otherwise one can begin to feel rather seasick.

TREE   At the conclusion of the Adagio [bar 161] we make no ritardando in preparation for the next variation:

We begin the Allegretto as though we ourselves are surprised. The quarter note of the Allegretto is very similar to the eighth note of the previous Adagio. It's the closest we come in this movement to "L'istesso tempo":

SOYER This variation is formed from two alternating ideas. The first four bars [162–165] consist of syncopated entrances forming chords; the next four [166–169] are built upon a figure of two eighth notes. Each of these ideas needs distinct characterization. In the first four bars we avoid accents on the syncopations and let the music unfold in one line, like an arpeggio played legato on the piano. In order to match the sonority of the first violin's open strings, we use very little vibrato.

STEINHARDT   In these four bars, rather than "phrasing" as such, we look for absolute equality of tone color in every entrance, including, of course, the lower voice played by each instrument. This passage takes on an almost otherworldly purity of sound.

TREE   In bars 166–169 we bring to the two-note figures a contrasting grazioso quality; we play with more vibrato, clear articulation, and rhythmic lilt. We regard the principal voices to be the eighth notes that change pitch, rather than the suspensions. Throughout the variation the principal voice is passed from player to player, giving a kaleidoscopic effect.

DALLEY   In the second part of the variation the contrasting colors alternate more rapidly:

We begin each two-bar phrase without vibrato and then vibrate where the hairpins are marked.

TREE   I used to feel that we weren't doing enough with this variation, that it was somewhat lacking in profile. And then I realized that its very effectiveness depends on its simplicity.

DALLEY   We now come to the extraordinary, hymnlike variation:

Beethoven marks "sotto voce"; later he indicates *p,* and later yet, *pp.* Is the "sotto voce" another way of expressing *p* or *pp*? This ambiguity in the use of the term "sotto voce" is found as well in the Cavatina of Opus 130. The songful nature of the Cavatina, although intimate, calls for a warm and expressive piano. In this variation we feel that the "sotto voce" has a more ethereal pianissimo quality.

STEINHARDT   The mood is hushed and sustained. The bow strokes are silken and floating, rather near the fingerboard, with no attempt to get "into the string." The ¾ should be felt in three beats per bar. Beethoven indicates "semplice," and this music—so inward and reverential—should be expressed as simply as possible.

TREE   The beautiful accents in the subsequent bars are conveyed mainly by the left hand:

STEINHARDT   Rather than increase the bow pressure for the accents, we increase the bow speed; this gives a more generous texture without really sounding louder. I would suggest beginning the crescendo in bar 191 not only very softly but with an extremely refined vibrato which intensifies as the phrase develops. In extending the crescendo through to the middle of bar 192, Beethoven lets the phrase open out like a flower:

DALLEY The way in which the voices are spaced here is reminiscent of Beethoven's keyboard writing; he will often have a thick chord in the bass and a wide interval in the treble. When we were students we were told to avoid that sort of doubling. But Beethoven didn't mind breaking the rules.

TREE At bar 195 the rumbling figure in the bass speaks ominously; there's something in the wind. . . .

SOYER The indication "non troppo marcato" cautions the cellist not to play with the forceful accentuation that will be required when the figure appears in forte [bar 203]. Even so, good left-hand articulation is needed. This is another case where bow and finger can, to advantage, strike the string simultaneously. Rhythmically, I don't think of the figure as foursquare but as a tight, compact unit.

At bar 203 the drama begins to unfold. Four times previously the cello figure has been heard without the other players' taking notice, and now, exaggerating the forte, I interrupt with a shout:

The others calm me down with their pianissimo, and I go on with my murmurings. But I become impatient again and, in bar 205, make another bid for attention.

TREE The three upper instruments want to achieve the utmost contrast to the outbursts in the cello. We are absolutely innocent and are terrified by what we've heard. In bar 203 we barely dare to play at all, doing so without vibrato in the lightest flautando. The dialogue between the by now villainous cello and the guileless upper voices seems almost operatic.

DALLEY These *pp* quarter notes built on augmented intervals have a less sustained, more hesitant quality than the quarters at the beginning of the variation; we therefore play them somewhat shorter. The passage is full of mystery.

SOYER At bar 211 the first violin finally responds to the cello's outburst with a forte of its own:

STEINHARDT In bars 220–226 there are five cadenzalike figures. Every one of these should be supple; I can't imagine a quartet playing them strictly in time. Each voice has something individual to contribute; the melodic curve comes in a different place. In keeping with the sotto voce I enter quietly with a light, airy sound and play my opening statement modestly, without much rubato:

The viola figure that follows is somewhat more dramatic; it traverses virtually the whole range of the instrument:

TREE   I give some rise and fall in dynamics to the two curves on which my phrase is built, but I have to be careful not to overdo these nuances. The subsequent cello passage [bar 224] has a printed crescendo and diminuendo and must therefore be able to rise to a greater height of intensity.

SOYER   I make an arc going to the high note, which I dwell on for an instant:

DALLEY   The second-violin figure seems to be the most complex of all:

I tend to elongate slightly both the high note (C sharp) and the expressively altered note (G natural). I judge whether to enter on a down- or an up-bow by the dynamic level at which Dave concludes his previous passage.

STEINHARDT   Either the cello or the second-violin passage could be considered the climactic point of the recitative. My last figure is, in any case, of less intensity:

I have to remember, however, not to arrive at the trill too softly; even though it's marked piano, it's followed by a further four bars of diminuendo:

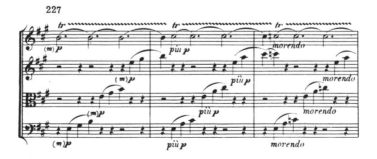

TREE   The diminuendo takes place not only in dynamics but in intensity. We begin in bar 227 with a rather full-throated *mp;* the sound then gradually becomes paler, with less and less vibrato, until, at bar 230, it falls away almost entirely. At the Allegretto the groups of eighth notes are led by the second violin and played with all up-bow spiccato strokes; this figure begins almost hesitatingly and takes on increasing vibrancy:

STEINHARDT   I prefer to bow across the bar line, just as I do in the original statement of the theme; otherwise there's a risk of getting a rather jerky effect. Beginning in bar 235 I use a hooked bowing to avoid inadvertent accents.

DALLEY   Beethoven could have given the first violin a free cadenza in bars 239–242, indicating "ad libitum." Instead he took great pains to place each note in a specific rhythmic context, thereby bringing about a kind of prepared spontaneity:

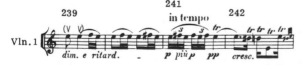

This concept of Beethoven's is extremely interesting. Such passages occur fairly frequently in his works, and when they do, the question arises: How much leeway is the interpreter permitted?

STEINHARDT   In bar 241 there are various ways of conceiving the relationship between the triplets and the trill. I play the triplets just as written and then start the trill itself rather slowly, as if beginning with faster triplets, blurring the rhythm for a moment. The effect is a kind of operatic approach to the trill. In bar 242 I play the note values exactly as written; this leaves me in good stead with my colleagues, who can enter happily in bar 243 without any doubt as to the tempo. After all the trading off of voices throughout the movement, the second violin and the viola finally take up the theme together to express their complete accord; the trills lend it wings:

TREE   These trills are also characteristic of Beethoven's keyboard writing. The cello figure (borrowed from the triads in bar 227) puts the stamp of a rustic dance on the passage. Accompaniment figures often do more to establish the character of a variation than thematic material which one has already heard.

SOYER   I play the three-note figure a little more rapidly than it's written. In this way it cuts through the texture more easily and gives added vitality to the rhythmic pulsation, which might otherwise be obscured by the trill and the legato melody.

TREE   In bars 250–253 we have another passage where several melodic segments have to be drawn into one line:

The three lower instruments must work together to make a gradual diminuendo spread over nine separate figures. Dave and I begin forte, not only to avoid being too soft too soon but to create a balance with the second violin, which is in a much higher register. Once we reach our softest point, in bar 252, we gradually build a crescendo over six separate figures.

The first-violin cadenza [bars 264–267] has more notes and is more brilliant than the previous recitativelike passages; it takes on a heroic quality:

In the concluding bars—as at the end of the second movement—all the stopping and starting creates its own sense of ritardando:

The falling figures seem to be sighing, almost pleading; the rests, weighing and considering. And how I love my long note—the E in bar 273—that one note in the midst of all the hesitations! The register is so beautiful, so dark and singing. It's telling us that we've arrived home.

STEINHARDT   The final bar [277] appears to be a typical place where the first violin would lead. But my bowed notes are, in fact, so soft and silvery that my leading would create difficulties for the three instruments playing pizzicato. So in this case John will lead and I'll just follow along.

SOYER   One of the main problems in interpreting this movement is to find just the right tempo relationships. Every variation, excepting the first, has both a change of time signature and a new tempo indication. This is a delicate matter and deserves a lot of thought. As we've mentioned, we don't believe that there need be common units of beats between the variations. The movement as a whole evolves more organically when the tempo relationships aren't set in arbitrary molds.

Fifth Movement

TREE   Now comes the romp! We regard the opening two bars as a curtain raiser—a sort of miniature overture. Dave plays as forcefully as he likes. His statement is terse and brusque, rather faster than the main tempo:

SOYER   It's as if I'm saying, "Pay attention, everybody—we're going to play this amazing scherzo!" And, by the way, one of the many surprising things about this scherzo is that it's in duple time. We think of the bar following my entrance more as a slight fermata than as a bar strictly in time.

STEINHARDT Extending the rest just a little longer than notated heightens the drama. After the cello's gruff exclamation it takes a moment before our timid souls dare talk back to the giant. By way of phrasing, we lean into the third bar of the theme [bar 5]:

In bar 4 one has to save the bow on the slurred notes so as to remain in its lower part for the sake of the spiccato. To set the forte notes in bar 9 more in relief, we make a little diminuendo just beforehand and play them on the string.

TREE At bar 25 we build the crescendo in tiers from voice to voice rather than within individual notes; each entrance is carefully gradated. The subsequent diminuendo then begins forte:

If the eighth-note upbeat enters too late at the Molto poco adagio, it will sound like a downbeat. To help ensure the metric sense we put a tiny accent on the first quarter-note B:

SOYER   When, at bar 37, Tempo primo returns, I don't break the slur. I use very little bow and catch the tempo immediately.

A ritardando is indicated in bar 44—but how much ritardando? It's very delicate from the ensemble standpoint:

The easiest solution is to take the whole bar in a slower tempo; but that doesn't do justice to Beethoven's intention. The ritardando should sound spontaneous—only gradually getting slower, not just an immediate meno mosso. Some years ago we came upon a wholly unexpected solution quite by accident. We were in the midst of rehearsing this passage—struggling over it without success—when Sonya Kroyt, the wife of Boris Kroyt, walked into the room. In her inimitable way she held out her arm regally and announced in her thick Russian accent, "Pleez don't get up. I hev cold. I'm not keessing anybodyeh." It suddenly struck us that the rhythm of her last sentence exactly suited the pace of the ritardando needed in this passage:

We tried it, and it worked like a charm. It was perfectly together, and we've used this stratagem ever since.★

STEINHARDT   The melody of the Trio is built in repetitive four-bar phrases:

★ Hearing the four Guarneri Quartet members tell this story is like seeing Kurosawa's film *Rashomon,* in which the same incident is described entirely differently by four observers. All four quartet players agree as to the relevance of the words in solving the musical problem. But at least three claim personal credit for having thought of the idea. To that effect Steinhardt advances his pre-eminence as "the clever one of the group"; Tree swears by an "Urtext version" which differs in some particulars from the above; and Dalley reluctantly admits, "It was my idea."

This can begin to sound monotonous if the accents always fall in the same place. In the first phrase we follow the melodic rise to the fourth bar [bar 72] and give a bit of spark to the B. In the second phrase we lean into the third bar [the F sharp in bar 75], the accent being lighter than in bar 72.

TREE   At bar 85 the juggling of voices—between viola and cello, then between the two violins—is notorious for its ensemble difficulty:

The only way to achieve at least approximate success with this passage is to anticipate every entrance. One must have the courage to risk playing too soon. Otherwise each entrance will sound late, and the line will be full of holes.

STEINHARDT   I try to remove from my mind any complications and concentrate on one simple element: the sense of the downbeats. The most difficult moment for me is when I take over from the viola in bar 89. If I wait to listen for the viola's last note I'll probably enter too late. Two or three bars before my entrance I have to establish within myself a feeling of when the viola's main beats arrive. For the sake of control, it's extremely important to keep the bow close to the string: you shouldn't have to *try* to bounce the bow; it should bounce by itself. I would suggest using very little arm or forearm movement and letting the motion come from the fingers.

TREE   I've sometimes wondered if Beethoven appreciated the man-hours in rehearsals that would be devoted to this passage over the centuries.

SOYER   Since Beethoven played the violin and viola himself, he must have realized that it would rarely sound quite right. But, after all, he could have written it for one instrument had he wished. I think he was playing a joke on the musicians and knew that it would sometimes come out with an irregular beat—a kind of three-footed humor.

STEINHARDT   By notating "Ritmo di quattro battute" in bar 109, Beethoven indicates that the four-bar phrase pattern begins two bars before the key change, and not—as could be misinterpreted—at the key change itself; his slurrings reinforce this idea:

DALLEY   The passage from bar 125 to bar 140 is particularly demanding for the second violin and the viola; the leaps are devilish, and the rhythm must, of course, remain consistent:

In bars 129–130 I use a fingering that avoids jumping across the strings. In bar 133 the low G sharp creates a major difficulty in that it forces you to stay in first position and then leap over to the A string for the C sharp [third note]. Reluctant as I am to omit or change notes, I consider it the lesser of two evils to leave out this G sharp rather than risk not playing the passage cleanly. Luckily, a G sharp is already established by the viola on the first beat, and the sound carries through.

TREE   If you were to listen to the viola line by itself, you'd think it was a work of the twentieth century. I approach this passage as a personal challenge. Clarity is the overriding consideration, and for that reason I prefer to remain in first (or half) position, no matter how awkward the string crossings may be.

SOYER   At bar 141 the figure in the upper voices has a comical air, and in keeping with this, one can bring to the bass a lightly lilting motion, with a touch of accent and diminuendo in each bar:

DALLEY   It's important to achieve equality of voices in the pizzicato passage:

For this reason I avoid playing my A on the open string. But the main problem is that the cello's pizzicato tends to sound far more resonant than the others'.

SOYER   This is a place where it's helpful for the cellist to dull the sound of the pizzicato a bit. My F sharp [bar 164] rings out so readily if played on the A string that I make a point of playing it on the D string. This fingering is a little more difficult from the standpoint of intonation, but one soon gets accustomed to it.

DALLEY   When, later in the movement, the pizzicato notes are immediately repeated by different instruments at the same pitch, the intonation needs special attention:

For instance, the D sharp [bar 329], being the leading note in E major, should be a shade high—but exactly how high? The G sharp in bar 332 would therefore be heard as a perfect fourth in relation to the D sharp. Obviously, the person who first plays the note sets the pitch. However, the tempo is so fast that it's hard to make adjustments on the spur of the moment. To some extent it's a question of chance, but you can help chance along by working out the intonation carefully in rehearsal.

TREE   The passage marked "sul ponticello" must have astonished Beethoven's public, just as Bartók's effects amazed listeners a hundred years later:

It's Dave's pet peeve when we rehearse this passage that we don't obtain enough ponticello color.

SOYER   One must really push the bow right up against the bridge to get that marvelous sound—like a little music box.

DALLEY   The ponticello color comes more easily if the spiccato strokes aren't too short; they should be brushed rather than pointed. If you try to make sure that every note speaks, you may not get enough ponticello in the sound. The effect of the ponticello is so startling, so new and so bold, that the actual notes—which have been heard many times before—are of less importance.

SOYER   From bar 479 onwards we take the two separate quarter notes up-bow. If we were to change the bow as it comes, the sound would be too heavy.

STEINHARDT   Then, at bar 487, the "sul ponticello" suddenly ceases:

It's as if you had a strange filter over a light which you quickly pull off, and it changes at once from one color to another.

At the conclusion of the movement the unexpected fall from E major to the octave G sharps has a jarring effect:

It's almost like earth tectonics—where a whole land mass shifts from one place to another. We hold the G sharps back to give them more weight.

Sixth Movement

STEINHARDT   We suddenly find ourselves drawn into the world of the Adagio. There's something almost manic-depressive about this. The wild excitement, the near-frenzy of the Scherzo go to an extreme in one direction. When that emotion has been totally spent, there's nowhere to go except the opposite pole. And what a dolorous, mournful piece it is!

TREE   This is, without doubt, one of the most moving passages in all music. What a moment for the viola!

Adagio quasi un poco andante.

Several commentators have drawn attention to the similarity between the first phrase of this theme and the Kol Nidre.* My colleagues doubt the relevance, but I believe that the similarity may not be entirely coincidental. After all, it's a historical fact that in 1825 the Viennese Jewish community had asked Beethoven to provide a cantata for the dedication of a new synagogue—a project which he contemplated but unfortunately never carried out. It's altogether possible that Beethoven came across the Kol Nidre while giving consideration to this project.

In any case, I start down-bow, because I want to be up-bow for the beginning of the melody [upbeat to bar 3].

DALLEY   The marking "Adagio quasi un poco andante" tells us that despite the slow tempo, a sense of motion is needed. The tempo is related

* See Paul Nettl, *A Beethoven Encyclopedia* (New York: Philosophical Library, 1956).

to the bowing; the long slurs are just about all the bow can sustain. With
the bow moving so slowly, I wouldn't play right over the fingerboard;
the resultant sound would be too white. Although it's piano, the tone
needs a certain degree of intensity.

TREE   In bars 11–14 the poignant falling figure expresses a real Welt-
schmerz if there ever was one:

We have to concur on the degree of rise and fall within the figure. This
is carried out more by the left hand than by the right. The diminuendo
in bar 25 shouldn't be interpreted in such a way as to bring about a
sudden decrease in volume. The arc of the phrase has to be preserved:

Arnold normally prepares for the Finale by making a little ritardando
during the last notes of the Adagio:

We are, however, watching John at this point.

DALLEY   In leading here, I relieve Arnold of the necessity of indicating
the *ff* attack for the Finale while placing his thirty-second note. But naturally, I try to sense just what he wants me to do.

Seventh Movement

SOYER   The Finale falls on us with a terrific turbulence:

Having already played for over half an hour with the intense concentration demanded throughout this work, to come to this wood-tearing, flesh-tearing movement has quite a vitalizing effect. I feel exhilarated, much as I do when playing the *Grosse Fuge*.

STEINHARDT   The first *ff* note comes as a shock. We play it right at the frog with a rapid, downward, hammerlike stroke. The question of tempo is of great importance. Nothing more than "Allegro" is marked. All the elements of the movement, including the lyrical second subject, are best served by a tempo that's not excessively fast. The piece sounds all the more powerful if it is unhurried; it's a kind of controlled madness. There's a rhythmic surge within the theme, both in the momentum of the eighths as they lean towards the quarters and in the momentum of the whole second bar as it goes towards the third, the pattern then being repeated. If the notes were beaten out on a drum, the rhythmic impulse would lead to the last quarter note of the phrase. Again Beethoven uses rests to create a heightening of impact.

TREE   We start the eighth-note figure down-bow and make a point of accenting the end of the stroke to give the necessary articulation to the quarter note. We then lift the bow and reattack the eighths.

DALLEY   I myself give particular attention to articulating the first eighth
in each group. The quarter notes have more length and can more easily
take care of themselves. The figure

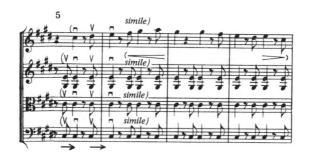

plays a major role in this movement, as it does in the Finale of Opus 59,
No. 2. There's always a close rhythmic relationship between the eighth
and the quarter. This is crucial to the life of the Finale and gives it a
ferocious energy. We bow this figure at least three different ways in this
movement, depending on the context. At bar 5, where it comes in *ff* and
should have as much power as possible, we play with up/down strokes
at the frog. A lot of right-hand finger motion gives bite to the stroke.

STEINHARDT   The phrasing follows the melodic rise and fall; there's a
kind of arc over each group of four bars. But the diminuendos are very
slight, for everything remains within the forte. As the second phrase
[bars 10–13] goes to a higher level, we increase the intensity.

SOYER   From bar 21 onwards the lyrical line must remain urgently expressive—it's feverish. There should be no sentimentalizing by slowing

down. We avoid bar-line accents; the viola maintains the rhythmic pulsation:

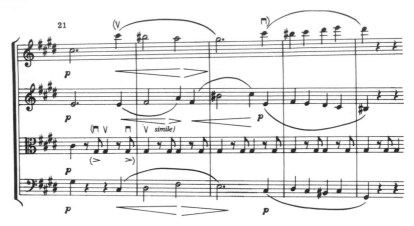

TREE   I play an iota more than piano—at the point, with a down/up bowing—and I make sure that the eighth is clearly heard. In other words, it's a case of deliberately accenting the "wrong" note.

DALLEY   At bar 40 *f* is indicated, as opposed to the *ff* at the beginning of the movement:

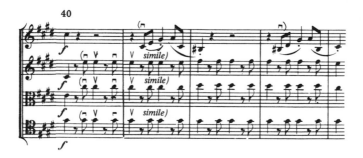

Beethoven is very particular about these markings, and the distinction always has to be respected. We therefore use the down/up bowing at the point, which has great vitality but is not quite so powerful as playing at the frog. We must take care not to cover the first violin, which plays the theme in a lower register than the three accompanying voices.

SOYER   With the arrival of the second subject, the relentless pounding of the rhythm relaxes. The sustained accompaniment allows more freedom. This exultant section welcomes a rhapsodic, improvisational approach:

STEINHARDT   I usually allow a little more time for the first three eighth notes and then cascade down towards the third bar. We take the liberty of interpreting the "poco ritenuto" as "poco ritardando." A strict ritenuto—a uniformly slower tempo—would be contrary to the natural suppleness of phrase which we think Beethoven had in mind. Even if nothing at all were marked, a good musician would probably feel something of a ritardando here.

DALLEY   The qualification "poco" is important. One wants to take a little time, and yet not overdo it. The rubato mustn't get out of hand.

TREE   As my phrase, beginning in bar 60, is an offshoot of Arnold's, I'll wait to see what he'll do. Normally I might lean into my second bar [bar 61] and make a little tenuto on the E. But if Arnold were to phrase his passage strongly in one way, I might on the spur of the moment decide to treat the rubato differently. This melody is so expressive that even if the same player were to repeat the phrase, he or she wouldn't want to play it twice in exactly the same way.

DALLEY   In bars 64 and 65 the second violin must sing out and the first violin play very piano. But then, in bars 66 and 67, even though the half notes are a continuation of the second violin's melody, they must be played with a restrained crescendo to let the first violin be heard:

STEINHARDT   If one has slightly held back the tempo for the second subject, the original tempo of the movement must absolutely be retaken at
bar 72; otherwise you'll find yourself in trouble six bars later:

It's interesting to see in the Breitkopf und Härtel edition of Beethoven's
collected works that within the second subject itself the indications of
"in tempo" which follow each "poco riten." appear in small print, but
at bar 72 the "in tempo" is in large print.

DALLEY   The passages of running eighth notes bring a specially light
and vivacious element into the Finale:

Where "non ligato" is marked, I like to begin with the bow a little off
the string and then play somewhat more on the string as the line descends and more power is needed.

SOYER In bars 160–164, where I play the motif *ff* in the lower register, the timbre of the C string manages to stand out in relief and come through the general texture:

Rather than pressing very hard, I use a lot of bow. Even if you don't get too much of the fundamental note, you'll get some swish to the bow stroke, and it will roar a bit. It's not the prettiest thing—but you don't want it to be pretty. Later, at bar 178, the cello has really to push through; it's a matter of brute force:

STEINHARDT In bar 337 the rhythmic motif appears again *ff*, but this time I use a hooked bowing to ensure that the strongest accent will fall on the sforzando at the beginning of each bar:

The *ff* is suddenly interrupted by a whispered fragment of the theme:

These notes should be strictly in tempo, taut and concise. But then comes one of those expressive rests: I don't look at it as a bar but as a space. The actual printed rhythmic value may be almost correct, but a moment is needed for the air to clear so that you can enter into the changed mood—quieter and more mysterious. At bar 350 the melody is taken by the first violin and the viola playing in octaves:

I let the timbre of the lower voice predominate. Mournful as the character may be, one should take care not to drag the tempo at this point. The presence of the fragment from the opening theme dictates a rhythmic vitality.

SOYER   This motif is reiterated almost as an idée fixe in the cello part, and, although piano, it creates a mood of intense agitation and should always be well articulated. Well, that is, in any case, my way of playing. Articulation is crucial to everything, even when playing "The Swan."

DALLEY   The tempo remains vital and the motif taut until bar 368, where we hold back a little, but without letting down the sense of expectancy:

One must be careful at this point not to be so slow as to anticipate the Poco adagio which comes ten bars later. And even there the tempo mustn't be excessively slow.

TREE   In the final bars the whole question of tempo needs careful consideration—not least the tempo of the last three chords. We've wrung our hands over them:

SOYER   Here you have the conclusion of this gigantic, stupendous work. If the final chords are played strictly in tempo, they sound almost frivolous. On the other hand, playing the chords with a strong ritenuto gives the impression of an entirely different tempo.

STEINHARDT   We've tried various solutions, such as elongating the rest and then playing the chords in tempo, or making an accelerando in bars 383–386 as the line rises and counterbalancing it with a final ritardando. None of these seems quite right.

SOYER   The upshot is that we play bars 383–386 fully in tempo, as marked, and then hold the chords back just a bit without robbing them of their brusque character.

DALLEY   The fact that Beethoven has written four-note chords for two of the instruments may in itself be an indication that he expected a little more time to be taken.

STEINHARDT   The Amadeus Quartet arpeggiates these chords broadly— admittedly a personal interpretation, but very effective. We break them only slightly.

SOYER   Whatever we do, we cannot escape the suddenness of the ending. A titanic power is abruptly brought to a halt. Beethoven has a final surprise for us: he concludes the work in C-sharp major. It's a fierce kind of affirmation. Maybe there's hope.

STEINHARDT   Let's not forget the fermata Beethoven has put over the final rest. I keep my bow poised for a moment in whatever position I'm in, so the listener knows that even though the last chords have sounded, the piece isn't quite finished.

Some comments about the Finale to Opus 131 elicited from the Guarneri Quartet members immediately after a performance, before they even had time to put down their instruments:

SOYER   It's savage—utterly savage—the culmination of the entire work.

DALLEY   Grotesque and wild! It has invincible energy.

TREE   A relentless dance, a demonic dance—and yet, what wonderfully tender moments, what an enormous emotional range!

STEINHARDT   He's shaking his fist at destiny. It's terrifying—but suddenly everything is released and it overflows with joy, with ecstasy.

DALLEY   You want to bark like a dog.

DISCOGRAPHY
GLOSSARY
INDEX

DISCOGRAPHY

This discography was compiled by Patrick Dillon, who would like to thank John Pfeiffer of RCA Records for his assistance.

The Guarneri Quartet records exclusively for RCA Red Seal Records.

  LP   12-inch long-playing record
 TC   tape cassette
 CD   compact disc
 OP   recording out of print as of publication of this book
   ★   originally released in both mono and stereo

The dates cited in parentheses indicate the year(s) of the recording sessions, not of the recording's release.

BARTÓK
The Six String Quartets (1974–76)
3 LP: ARL 3-2412

BEETHOVEN
The Complete String Quartets (1966–69)
11 LP: VCS 11-100 (OP)

The Six Early Quartets, Opus 18 (1969)
3 LP: VCS 6195 (OP)

The Five Middle Quartets, Opus 59 ("Razumovsky"), Opus 74, Opus 95 (1966–68)
4 LP: VCS 5415★

The Five Late Quartets, Opus 127, Opus 130, Opus 131, Opus 132,
      Opus 135; *Grosse Fuge,* Opus 133 (1968–69)
4 LP: VCS 6418

Quartet in F, Opus 59, No. 1 ("Razumovsky") (1967)
LP: LSC 3286 (OP)

Quartet in E minor, Opus 59, No. 2 ("Razumovsky") (1966)
LP: LSC 3287 (OP)

Quartets, in C, Opus 59, No. 3 ("Razumovsky") (1966); in E flat,
      Opus 74 ("Harp") (1968)
LC: LSC 3288 (OP)

String Quintet in C, Opus 29 (Pinchas Zukerman, viola) (1978)
      (w. Mendelssohn: Quintet in B flat, Opus 87)
LP: ARL1-3354   TC: ARK1-3354

BORODIN
Quartet No. 2 in D (1978, 1980) (w. Dohnányi: Quartet No. 2 in D flat)
LP: ARL1-4331   TC: ARK1-4331

BRAHMS
The Complete String Quartets (1974, 1978–79) (w. Schumann:
      Complete Quartets)
3 LP: ARL3-3834   3 TC: ARK3-3834

The Two String Quintets (Pinchas Zukerman, viola) (1983)
LP: ARC1-4849   TC: ARE1-4849

Piano Quintet in F minor, Opus 34 (Arthur Rubinstein, piano) (1966)
LP: LSC 2971

The Three Piano Quartets (Arthur Rubinstein, piano) (1967)
      (w. Schumann: Piano Quintet in E flat, Opus 44)
3 LP: LSC 6188

DEBUSSY
Quartet (1973) (w. Ravel: Quartet)
LP: ARL1-0187 (OP)

DOHNÁNYI
Quartet No. 2 in D flat, Opus 15 (1980) (w. Borodin: Quartet No. 2 in D)
LP: ARL1-4331   TC: ARK1-4331

DVOŘÁK
Piano Quintet, Opus 81 (Arthur Rubinstein, piano) (1971)
LP: LSC 3252 (OP); AGL1-4882

Quartet No. 11 in C, Opus 61; Terzetto, Opus 74 (1972)
LP: ARL1-0082 (OP)

Quartet No. 12 in F, Opus 96 ("American") (1972); String Quintet No. 3
in E flat, Opus 97 (Walter Trampler, viola) (1975)
LP: ARL1-1791   TC: ARK1-1791

Quartet No. 13 in G, Opus 106 (1979)
LP: ARL1-4051   TC: ARK1-4051

Quartet No. 14 in A flat, Opus 105 (w. Smetana: Quartet in E minor) (1965)
LP: LSC 2887* (OP)

FAURÉ
Quartet, Opus 121 (1973); Piano Quartet in C minor, Opus 15 (Arthur
Rubinstein, piano) (1970)
LP: ARL1-0761 (OP); AGL1-4876

GRIEG
Quartet in G minor, Opus 27 (1966) (w. Mendelssohn: Quartet in
A minor, Opus 13)
LP: LSC 2948* (OP)

HAYDN
Quartets, Opus 20, No. 4 in D (1974); Opus 74, No. 3 in G minor (1970)
LP: ARL1-3485   TC: ARK1-3485

Quartets, Opus 77, No. 1 in G; No. 2 in F (1977)
LP: ARL1-2791 (OP); AGL1-4898   TC: ARK1-2791 (OP); AGK1-4898

MENDELSSOHN
Quartet in A minor, Opus 13 (1966) (w. Grieg: Quartet in G minor, Opus 27)
LP: LSC 2948* (OP)

Quintet in B flat, Opus 87 (Pinchas Zukerman, viola) (1978) (w. Beethoven:
Quintet in C, Opus 29)
LP: ARL1-3354   TC: ARK1-3354

MOZART
Eine kleine Nachtmusik, K. 525 (Julius Levine, double bass) (1980) (w. Schubert:
Quintet in A, Opus 114)
LP: ARC1-5167   TC: ARE1-5167   CD: RCD-5167

The Complete Piano Quartets (Arthur Rubinstein, piano) (1971)
LP: ARL1-2676   TC: ARK1-2676

Quartets in B flat, K. 589; in F, K. 590 (1965)
LP: LSC 2888* (OP)

Six Quartets Dedicated to Haydn, Nos. 14–19 (1971–74)
3 LP: CRL3-1988 (OP)

Volume 1: No. 14 in G, K. 387 (1974); No. 15 in D minor, K. 421 (1971)
LP: ARL1-0760 (OP)

Volume 2: No. 16 in E, K. 428; No. 17 in B flat, K. 458 ("Hunt") (1973)
LP: ARL1-0762

Volume 3: No. 18 in A, K. 464 (1975); No. 19 in C, K. 465 ("Dissonant") (1974)
LP: ARL1-1153 (OP); AGL1-4908   TC: ARK1-1153 (OP); AGK1-4908

Quartets, No. 20 in D, K. 499 (1973); No. 21 in D, K. 575 (1970)
LP: ARL1-4687   TC: ARK1-4687

The Complete String Quintets (Ida Kavafian, Steven Tenenbom,
    Kim Kashkashian, viola) (1984–85)
3 LP (release forthcoming)

RAVEL
Quartet (1973) (w. Debussy: Quartet)
LP: ARL1-0187 (OP)

SCHUBERT
Quartets, No. 13 in A minor, D. 804 (1971); No. 12 in C minor
    ("Quartettsatz") (1970)
LP: LSC 3285 (OP)

Quartet No. 14 in D minor, D. 810 ("Death and the Maiden") (1976)
    (w. Wolf: Italian Serenade)
LP: ARL1-1994 (OP); AGL1-4928   TC: ARK1-1994 (OP); AGK1-4928

Quartet No. 15 in G, D. 887 (1977)
LP: ARL1-3003

Quintet in A, D. 667 ("Trout") (Emanuel Ax, piano; Julius Levine, double bass)
    (1983) (w. Mozart: *Eine kleine Nachtmusik*)
LP: ARC1-5167   TC: ARE1-5167   CD: RCD-5167

Quintet in C, D. 956 (Leonard Rose, cello) (1975)
LP: ARL1-1154 (OP)   TC: ARK1-1154 (OP)

SCHUMANN
The Complete String Quartets (1977–79) (w. Brahms: Complete Quartets)
3 LP: ARL3-3834

SMETANA

Quartet in E minor ("From My Life") (1965) (w. Dvořák: Quartet
    in A flat, Opus 105)
LP: LSC 2887★ (OP)

TCHAIKOVSKY

Quartet No. 1 in D, Opus 11 (1983) (w. Verdi: Quartet in E minor)
LP: ARL1-5419   TC: ARK1-5419

Sextet, Opus 70 ("Souvenir de Florence") (Boris Kroyt, viola; Mischa
    Schneider, cello) (1965)
LP: LSC 2916★ (OP)

VERDI

Quartet in E minor (1982) (w. Tchaikovsky: Quartet No. 1 in D)
LP: ARL1-5419   TC: ARK1-5419

WOLF

Italian Serenade (1976) (w. Schubert: Quartet No. 14 in D minor)
LP: ARL1-1994 (OP); AGL1-4928   TC: ARK1-1994 (OP); AGK1-4928

GLOSSARY OF
STRING-PLAYING TERMS

Arco   The bow. *Coll'arco.* Playing with the bow, as opposed to pizzicato.

Bridge   The arched piece of wood that supports the strings and transmits their vibrations to the body of the instrument.

Collé   A stroke in which the bow grips the string as in staccato, but initiated from off the string.

Détaché   A stroke in which a separate bow is taken for each note; the bow remains on the string.

Double-stop   Two notes played simultaneously.

Down-bow   Drawing the bow in the direction from frog to point.

F-holes   The two F-shaped outlets, or sound holes, cut in the belly of the instrument.

Fingerboard   The ebony board against which the strings are pressed by the fingers.

Flautando   Drawing the bow lightly and rapidly over the strings (usually near the fingerboard) to produce a flutelike timbre.

Frog (heel)   The heaviest part of the bow, held under the hand.

Glissando   An audible shift produced by sliding the finger along the string from one note to another.

Harmonics   Overtones (or upper partial tones) of ethereal or silvery timbre, produced when a string is lightly touched at certain mathematically prescribed points, rather than being "stopped" in the usual way.

Hooked bowing   The playing of two or more separated notes without change of bow direction.

Legato   Smoothly connecting one note to another.

Lower part of the bow   The section between the middle and the frog.

Martelé   "Hammered"; a bow stroke that begins with an incisive accent.

Nut   The ridge over which the strings pass at the head end of the fingerboard. (In England the term is also used to refer to the heel, or frog, of the bow.)

Off the string   Using a stroke in which the bow leaves the string between notes, e.g., spiccato.

On the string   Using a stroke in which the bow remains on the string between notes, e.g., détaché.

Open string   A string that is bowed or plucked without any finger being pressed upon it, thus vibrating in its whole length.

Pizzicato   Plucking the string.

Point (tip)   The lightest part of the bow, at the opposite end from the frog (or heel).

Ponticello   The bridge. *Sul ponticello*. Playing with the bow very near the bridge, thereby greatly diminishing the lower overtones in favor of the higher, with a resultant thin, eerie, whistling sound.

Portato   Gently separating one note from another.

Position   The specific placement of the hand on the fingerboard, the "first position" being the lowest, the subsequent positions rising higher on the fingerboard. One can often choose between playing a given passage in a low position on a high string or in a high position on a low string.

Sautillé   A springing bow stroke executed rapidly, the hair barely leaving the string.

Scordatura   A deliberate mistuning of one or more strings so as to facilitate some type of passage or alter the general tonal effect.

Shift   The movement of the left hand from one position to another.

Spiccato   A bouncing stroke, usually executed in the lower or middle part of the bow.

Staccato   A series of short, quick, martelé strokes, differing from spiccato in that the bow hair does not leave the string between strokes.

Stopped note   A note that is created by placing a finger on a string, as distinguished from playing an open string.

Up-bow   Drawing the bow in the direction from point to frog.

Upper part of the bow   The section between the middle and the point.

Vibrato   An oscillation of the finger on the string; variable in width and speed.

Viola (alto) clef

Wolf A breaking of sound that sometimes occurs when, owing to inherent structural factors, certain notes cause the body of the instrument to resonate excessively. On the cello the F on the G string is often a "wolf" note.

INDEX

A Note About the Author

David Blum is known both as a conductor and as an author on musical subjects. Born in 1935, he received his musical training in his native Los Angeles and in Europe. In 1961 he founded and conducted New York's Esterhazy Orchestra. His recordings of Haydn symphonies with that ensemble and of Mozart works with the English Chamber Orchestra have received international acclaim. David Blum now lives in Switzerland, directs the Orchestre Symphonique Genevois, and guest conducts in Europe. His books, which have been translated into many languages, include *Casals and the Art of Interpretation*.

A Note on the Type

The text of this book was set in a digitized version of Bembo, a well-known Monotype face. Named for Pietro Bembo, the celebrated Renaissance writer and humanist scholar who was made a cardinal and served as secretary to Pope Leo X, the original cutting of Bembo was made by Francesco Griffo of Bologna only a few years after Columbus discovered America.

Sturdy, well-balanced, and finely proportioned, Bembo is a face of rare beauty, extremely legible in all of its sizes.

Composed by Graphic Composition, Inc.
Athens, Georgia

Printed and bound by Fairfield Graphics,
Fairfield, Pennsylvania